Rodica Panta

Models of contemporary public diplomacy

Rodica Panta

Models of contemporary public diplomacy

LAP LAMBERT Academic Publishing

Impressum / Imprint

Bibliografische Information der Deutschen Nationalbibliothek: Die Deutsche Nationalbibliothek verzeichnet diese Publikation in der Deutschen Nationalbibliografie; detaillierte bibliografische Daten sind im Internet über http://dnb.d-nb.de abrufbar.

Alle in diesem Buch genannten Marken und Produktnamen unterliegen warenzeichen-, marken- oder patentrechtlichem Schutz bzw. sind Warenzeichen oder eingetragene Warenzeichen der jeweiligen Inhaber. Die Wiedergabe von Marken, Produktnamen, Gebrauchsnamen, Handelsnamen, Warenbezeichnungen u.s.w. in diesem Werk berechtigt auch ohne besondere Kennzeichnung nicht zu der Annahme, dass solche Namen im Sinne der Warenzeichen- und Markenschutzgesetzgebung als frei zu betrachten wären und daher von jedermann benutzt werden dürften.

Bibliographic information published by the Deutsche Nationalbibliothek: The Deutsche Nationalbibliothek lists this publication in the Deutsche Nationalbibliografie; detailed bibliographic data are available in the Internet at http://dnb.d-nb.de.

Any brand names and product names mentioned in this book are subject to trademark, brand or patent protection and are trademarks or registered trademarks of their respective holders. The use of brand names, product names, common names, trade names, product descriptions etc. even without a particular marking in this work is in no way to be construed to mean that such names may be regarded as unrestricted in respect of trademark and brand protection legislation and could thus be used by anyone.

Coverbild / Cover image: www.ingimage.com

Verlag / Publisher:
LAP LAMBERT Academic Publishing
ist ein Imprint der / is a trademark of
OmniScriptum GmbH & Co. KG
Heinrich-Böcking-Str. 6-8, 66121 Saarbrücken, Deutschland / Germany
Email: info@lap-publishing.com

Herstellung: siehe letzte Seite /
Printed at: see last page
ISBN: 978-3-659-68480-7

Table of content:

1. Public diplomacy - foreign policy instrument

The contemporary international environment is a global communications environment, which becomes more and more complex, more affordable and more democratized. Within the globalization, this one has had important transformations, which were noticed in the way of communication at the global level, due to the revolution in the media, but also to the appearance of many international actors with an increasing role in the world politics.

The Internet has globally confused the way of communication, the world governments being determined to search various ways of communication with the foreign public, in order to promote its national interests, to strengthen the old alliances and create new partnerships with the world States. Owing to the democratization and the world markets opening, nowadays world is an interconnected world, where, an increasing number of people has access to information, and implicitly, the possibility to participate in decisions making within the internal and foreign policy.

Foreign policy, previously an area managed exclusively by diplomats behind closed doors, is increasingly democratized. Ordinary citizens, NGOs, national ministries, private companies, academicians and other actors are directly involved in the foreign policy through public debate aimed at foreign policy issues. In an international environment previously dominated by tools of persuasion and coercion, the information exchange and its attractiveness as essential elements for the development of the "soft power", stand out increasingly[1].

The public diplomacy, both as a science, and as an activity, represents the modality to understand the state policy from the perspective of its interaction with the societies of other nations, or the influence on the foreign public opinion. This form of contemporary diplomacy refers to the influence of the public attitudes in the formation and execution of foreign policy, including the dimensions of the international relations which go beyond the traditional diplomacy, such as, the propagation of the public opinion from other countries by the governments, the

---

[1] R. Panta. Public diplomacy - foreign policy instrument. In: Agora, Vol VI, 2012, nr. 1, p. 54.

interaction with private or interest groups from other states, the communication with those involved in the international communication process.

Today, the credibility and the image the states projected are crucial components of their foreign policy; because these form "their soft power policy". The credibility of a State to members of the international society (states, international institutions, companies and NGOs) depends, among other things, on the ability to listen and be heard, and a tool that meets the needs of states to create "soft power" is the *public diplomacy*.

Even though the concept of *public diplomacy* is used almost half a century, both the practitioners and the theorists, continue to contradict regarding its exact definition. Until nowadays, the notion of public diplomacy constitutes the topic of some theoretical and normative debates, being subject to the scientific and diplomatic analysis.

Most researchers consider Edmund Guillon, the author of the contemporary "public diplomacy" term. The career diplomat used the phrase in 1965, in connection with the establishment of the Edward R. Murrow Center within Tuft University, Faculty of Law and Diplomacy.

We can divide public diplomacy historiography in two periods - before and after Guillon. Before Guillon, defining public diplomacy focused on its concretization. At the same time, research has been focused on discussing what is and what not public diplomacy is. From this perspective, a few groups of specialists which set the development of the academic and practical discourse of the contemporary public diplomacy may be mentioned.

The term was defined by Edmund Guillon - "the influence of public attitudes in the formation and execution of foreign policy, within the informational material of the Center. It encompasses dimensions of international relations beyond traditional diplomacy ... [Including] government's formation of public opinion of other countries, interaction between private interest groups from different countries, informing the public on international affairs and their influence on domestic policy, communication between those whose function is communication, such as diplomats and foreign journalists , (and) the process of intercultural communication"[2].

After Guillon particular attention is given to interpretation of the concept of public diplomacy, soft power and its relations with its influence on social relations, the

---

[2] I. Guceac, S. Porcescu. Diplomatia publica – componenta indispensabila a discursului extern in conditiile globalizarii. In: Akademos, martie 2010, nr. 1(16), p. 6.

relationship between national branding and public diplomacy, public diplomacy role in contemporary international relations.

To better understand the public diplomacy, it is necessary to compare it with the traditional diplomacy, explaining the first element from the expression of the *public diplomacy*.

Even though the term of *diplomacy* had been used in English since 1645, it has a multitude of definitions. Up to now, the term continues to be subject of many debates, which propose to establish what exactly the diplomacy is: a science or an art? The majority of scientists opts for both characteristics, attaching that of activity, explaining thus the complexity of the notion of diplomacy: as *a science*, the diplomacy delivers ideas, concepts, principles and rules, concerning the administration of the international relations; as *an art*, it offers us modalities, skills and abilities to make, in the best conditions, the orientations of foreign policy; as *an activity*, the diplomacy works exactly through its specific means, especially the negotiations, in order to implement the policy of the state[3].

In contrast with the foreign policy, which is generally expressed in public, mostly, the *diplomacy* is directed in secret, even though the results are made publicly in the contemporary international relations.

The public diplomacy fulfills the main function of the traditional diplomacy – it defends the state interests through peaceful means, the most often, through communication. They don't address to the official representatives of a sovereign power, but to the population in order to obtain their political understanding and support. Unlike its traditional objectives, the public diplomacy has a crucial purpose, to ameliorate or rectify the national image.

The foregoing allows us to conclude that the public diplomacy differs from the traditional diplomacy by the fact that public diplomacy deals not only with governments, but especially with individuals and non-governmental organizations.

Furthermore, public diplomacy activities often present different views, representing not only government' positions but also those of the citizens, engaging diverse and numerous non-governmental elements of a society[4].

The population can be influenced through public diplomacy activities by broadcasting a message, some ideas or information, in order to convince the target

---

[3] P. Tănăsie. Uzanţe diplomatice şi de protocol. Piteşti: Independenţa economică, 2000. p. 5.
[4] R. Shaum. Noua diplomatie. Relatii internationale moderne. Bucuresti: Antet, 2004. 136 p.

audience. This definition, from an etymological perspective, establishes a logical connection between the public diplomacy and the propaganda.

The propaganda represents a group of people using any kind of communication capabilities which influence the attitude or the behavior of another group of people. This definition recognizes the existence of the two mandatory elements, presented within the propaganda: *the information* and *the information purpose* – for modifying attitudes and behaviors. Both elements are characteristic to the public diplomacy, but there are more conditions which the public diplomacy has to accomplish in order to be clearly differentiated by propaganda. According to Mark Leonard's conception, the most important is the realization and the maintaining of a bidirectional flux of information[5]. This thing became more evident after September 11th 2001, when it was observed the aversion toward what was perceived as a flux of unidirectional culture, from the Western states to the rest of the world, being necessary of an inversely informational flux, from the rest of the world to the Western states.

Definitions of public diplomacy, presented above, are generally accepted by academic circles, but it also remains a contested term, because so far, there is no consensus regarding its definition or goals pursued[6]. Its equivocal feature can be explained by the multidisciplinary nature of the term. This is because public diplomacy is not an exclusively political concept; it is the intersection of several areas: communication, international marketing, and international relations etc.

Joseph Nye, published in 1990 *Bound to Lead*, in which the author develops the notion of "soft power". The author, concerned about the decline of the American power following the disappearance of the Soviet threat, has determined that the nature of state power is transformed and that the U.S. should use the second facet of power – "soft power". This change of the nature of power comes from the inability to calculate it only in terms of resources, population, territory, natural resources, military strength, social stability, economic level, but also the ability to change the behavior of other states[7].

"Hard power" is the pressure, inducement, military or economic threats imposed by a state to get something, while "soft power" is materialized by the fact that someone else wants to do what we want. Rallying capacity is not equivalent to the

---

[5] M. Leonard, C. Stead, C. Smewing. Public Diplomacy. London: The Foreign Policy Centre, 2002. http://fpc.org.uk/fsblob/35.pdf. (accessed 8.10.13)

[6] M. Devirieux. Étude et critique du concept de diplomatie publique. In : Jurnal of Policy Studies, winter, 2011. p. 61.

[7] R. Panta. Public diplomacy- foreign policy instrument. In: Agora, Vol VI, 2012, nr. 1, p. 55.

concept of influence because it can also prevent economic pressure or military "hard power". The last refers to a relationship of control, while the first leads to cooperative behavior. A country has three sources of "soft power": the first comes from culture, values and internal policies, or its foreign policy style and essence[8] . Culture, as the same author argues, can be divided into two categories: popular culture and what Nye called "high culture" - ballet, opera, painting. When this culture is admired and includes universal values and interests, it constitutes a source of "soft power".

Often considered a tool of public diplomacy, cultural diplomacy is the domain of diplomacy aimed at establishing, developing and sustaining relationships with other countries through culture, arts, education and science. Being a exterior projection of the cultural values of a state and the its promotion to the level of bilateral and multilateral relations, cultural diplomacy aims to support relations with other countries through culture, education and science; open alternative ways of communication to the public of the residence country, cultivate and initiate (if needed) long-term cultural relations between states; exercise influence in supporting foreign policy priorities; to use the tools of cultural diplomacy to promote economic interests.

Cultural diplomacy is, on the one hand, the sign of maturity, economic and political power of a state, but also a good barometer of the intensity and sincerity of relations between states that practice it. Researchers in the field of cultural diplomacy emphasize the difference between public and cultural diplomacy in that first is oriented toward short-term information dissemination and to promote policies; and the cultural - to establish long term relationships. Public diplomacy as traditionally perceived includes government support programs in the cultural, educational and informational fields, citizen exchange and programs aimed at informing and influencing the foreign audience[9].

A veritable instrument of the state's politics, culture often attenuates the tensions which manifest themselves in the interstate rapports, but the discipline of the international relations mentioned the culture importance for understanding and explaining the political phenomen and international strategies[10].

---

[8] J. Nye. Soft Power: The means to success in world politics. New York: Public Affairs, 2004. 208 p.
[9] I. Guceac S. Porcescu. Diplomatia publica – componenta indispensabila a discursului extern in conditiile globalizarii. In: Akademos, martie 2010, nr. 1(16), p. 7.
[10] C. Conte. La diplomatie culturelle française: La culture face à de nouveaux enjeux ? Toulouse: IEP, 2008. p.12, http://www.interarts.net/descargas/interarts678.pdf. (accessed 18.05.13)

The explication of the public diplomacy concept would be incompletely without its perceiving from the specialists perspective from territorial marketing who have as a study main objective the concept of commercialization of the state (nation – branding). The term *branding* denotes the organization, commercialization and communication activity of the brand name and identity, in order to ameliorate its reputation. *Nation branding* means the same thing, but at the country level.

The common point between the nation branding and the public diplomacy is the necessity to consolidate the national identity in a global international environment. The strategies of public diplomacy are linked to the state apparatus, but those of nation branding are assured by marketing agencies.

There are some ways to analyze the rapport between the public diplomacy and the nation branding: the public diplomacy is an integral part of the conception of nation branding; the conception of nation branding is a component part of public diplomacy (it is considered an instrument of the public diplomacy or its economic dimension)[11].

Even though these two conceptions are different, they partially coincide, due to the existence of the common points: culture, identity, image, values. We mention that the concepts of nation branding and public diplomacy have two common interests and the same action field – both aims to create a positive image of the state and to promote it abroad.

There are several ways of analyzing public diplomacy. We think that one of the best was proposed by Bruce Gregory, Director of "George Washington" University Institute of Public Diplomacy. He proposed three ways of analyzing public diplomacy[12], we used in analyzing models below.

First - *public diplomacy is an instrument of state acting in three temporal cycles*: 1. the media and continuous abundance of information, 2. public diplomacy campaign that can take months or years, as it addresses sensitive issues, 3. public diplomacy is used as a long term commitment (which was not present during the Cold War). A public diplomacy campaign to be successful must build bridges between peoples of the world and their institutions. The best instruments for success

---

[11] G. Szondi. Public Diplomacy and Nation Branding, Conceptual Similarities and Differences (Discussion Papers in Diplomacy), Netherlands Institute of International Relations „Clingendael". peacepalacelibrary.nl (accessed 16.04.14)

[12] B.Gregory. Not Your Grandparent's Public Diplomacy (Ottawa : Public Diplomacy Retreat Department of Foreign Affairs, November 30, 2005). p. 5-7 https://www.gwu.edu/~smpa/faculty/documents/PDRetreat_000.pdf (accessed 16.04.14)

are exchange programs between universities and, involving the artists[13]. These methods provide different results depending on the country. These dimensions of public diplomacy are instrumental, serving different interests of each state and, public diplomacy has its limits within each of them.

A second way of conceptualizing, in accordance with the opinion of Bruce Gregory is to consider *public diplomacy in the service of the state*. In other words public diplomacy is a government instrument of multiple components. The reason for this comes from multidisciplinary character and proximity to public diplomacy. A different department uses the concept under another name, such as: cultural diplomacy, international marketing, informing, military operations, etc.

The third analysis method of public diplomacy, proposed by Bruce Gregory is the *importance of the national sphere in foreign affairs*. Often, it is considered wrong that the Department of Foreign Affairs is a separate entity from the foreign affairs, but the separation between the two areas is purely mechanical and impermeable. Exponents of neorealist school consider, both spheres influence each other and are interdependent. For this reason we can say that public diplomacy has an internal dimension. Foreign policy of the state must be supported by citizens.

To get public support of citizens, foreign affairs departments must develop the potential of its society through universities, business communities and NGOs. In the XXI century, Ministry of Foreign Affairs of all States, should act not only internationally but at the national level also. In this aspect, many researchers find the link between public affairs and public diplomacy. Ministry of Foreign Affairs, for a successful foreign policy campaign act not only internationally but also domestically.

In most countries the public diplomacy activities are involved not only Ministry of Foreign Affairs, but also Ministry of Defense, Ministry of Tourism, Ministry of Economy Ministry of Culture etc. Each of these institutions offers different purposes of public diplomacy: political, economic and cultural. They must cooperate with each other to ensure the achievement of the public diplomacy strategy.

The public diplomacy has not changed during the last years. It modified the international context by increasing the importance of public opinion, the democracy exportation, the ascension of international environments, the augmentation of Diaspora, a vaster definition of security, the worldwide communications progress, which impose the necessity of a transparence (this event is also linked to the

---

[13] M. Devirieux. Étude et critique du concept de diplomatie publique. In : Jurnal of Policy Studies, winter, 2011. p. 63.

involvement of the civil society in the international political field), the culture globalization (attracted the will to protect the culture diversity) and the alteration of the concept ,,state power''. All these changes have transformed the public diplomacy in an important instrument of realization of national interests of the States.

In the middle of the first decade of the 21st century, the scientists use the notion *the new public diplomacy*. This resumed all the evolutionary and revolutionary modifications which appeared within the public diplomacy, but also to confirm the differences between the external communication systems during the Cold War with those during the third millennium[14].

This new form of contemporary diplomacy includes the following elements: it is promoted by the state and non-state actors (for example, by the NGOs); it relies on the *soft power*, the bidirectional communication, the strategic public diplomacy, the information administration, the country branding and the virtual image on Internet *(e – image)*; it involves the external policy adaptation and deals with both, the short and long – term problems[15].

One of the factors, that conditioned the appearance of the notion *new public diplomacy*, represents the development of the new communication technologies, especially the Internet, which has extended the communication skills of the non – state actors.

After the events of 11 September 2001, public diplomacy has become an important area of research. The current paradigm of public diplomacy research is international communication, which takes place at three levels: interpersonal, interstate and through information technologies. Each of these levels explains complexity of the public diplomacy activities. At interpersonal level, people play an important role individually or in various groups, interstate - in accordance with traditional diplomacy and through information technologies which provides ways of influencing the public opinion.

---

[14] E. Gilboa Public Diplomacy in the Information Age. http://icp-forum.gr/wp/wp-content/uploads/2008/12/gilboa-lecture-athens-jan-2009.pdf. (accessed 18.12.13)
[15] E. Gilboa Public Diplomacy in the Information Age. http://icp-forum.gr/wp/wp-content/uploads/2008/12/gilboa-lecture-athens-jan-2009.pdf. (accessed 18.12.13)

2. The origin and evolution of the U.S. public diplomacy

Although the public diplomacy has emerged as a consequence of the substantial changes that occurred in the world politics in the late 20th century and early 21st century, both its origins and its main development trends originate from the foreign policy applied by the United States during the last century. The term public diplomacy was coined and put into practice in the Unites States during the Cold War and, it time; it was taken over by other countries.

The beginning of the prehistory of U.S. public diplomacy dates back to the work of the Founding Fathers of the United States[16]. The history of both traditional and public diplomacies, just as the history of the U.S. diplomacy, has its origins in the Declaration of Independence of July 4, 1776. After the independence had been proclaimed, the major issue of the U.S. diplomacy consisted in the international acknowledgement of the United States by other countries. Such achievement depended on the way the American cause would be explained to other countries.

As a representative elected to promote the U.S. national interests, Benjamin Franklin enjoyed an obvious success in Europe by that time[17]. He did not confine his intense diplomatic work to British and French courts and governments. Furthermore, he traveled to London and Paris in order to present the case of his country to the British and French peoples[18]; he published a great number of documents, articles and essays in the British newspapers in a bid to create the impression that the American colonies have supporters.

The U.S. public diplomacy emerged as a government activity during World War I, at the same time as the Committee on Public Information (CPI) was established. The chairman of the CPI, George Creel, published articles about war in newspapers and prepared publications and posters to be spread to the general public. The purpose of the CPI was to use various newspapers and publications available to the American public as a means to support the decision of the U.S. President W. Wilson of abandoning the Monroe Doctrine ("America for the Americans") and getting the United States involved in the war.

---

[16]I. Galal. The History and Future of US Public Diplomacy. In: Global Media Journal, 2005, vol. 4. http://lass.purduecal.edu/cca/gmj/fa05/graduatefa05/gmj-fa05gradinv-galal.htm (accessed 12.01.14).
[17] D. Mazilu. Dreptul diplomatic si consular. București: Lumina Lex, 2009. p. 149.
[18] A. A. Bardos. Public diplomacy: An old art, a new profession. In: Virginia Quarterly Review, 2001, 77 (3) p. 426.

The United States' entry into World War II was a landmark event in the history of the U.S. public diplomacy[19]. In June 1942, the United States Office of War Information (OWI) was established in order to counterweigh Nazi propaganda and the then existing psychological war. Given the influence of the war situation, the U.S. public diplomacy in the period of the years 1942-1945 was a tool of external policy, which was created to suit the war-time demands.

The missions of these two agencies – the Committee on Public Information (CPI) and the United States Office of War Information (OWI) – were nearly identical, that is, to disseminate pro-American and pro-ally information and thus to contribute to the victory over the Axis and to the promotion of the American-style democracy worldwide[20]. Until today, promotion of the American-style democracy worldwide is a constant objective of US public diplomacy.

The history of U.S. public diplomacy in the 20th century can be divided in three stages. Each of those three stages has some key characteristics, as they all unfolded in specific junctures.

The first period covers an interval of four years and is considered to be the Golden Age of U.S. public diplomacy. It began in the 1950s and was characterized by the dissemination of the American and Western values and principles in the Eastern Europe in the context of the Cold War. The United States Information Agency (USIA)[21] is the first agency having officially declared the mission of coordinating U.S. public diplomacy. According to some researchers, the Soviet Union was defeated mainly ideologically during the Cold War, in terms of propaganda and public diplomacy, thanks to the efforts of the USIA.

Established in 1953 during the presidency of Eisenhower, the USIA became an efficient tool for promoting the American ideology aimed at fighting the communism. The work of this agency also marked the strongest effort ever made by a society to influence the attitudes and behaviors of people outside its borders. The USIA's mission was to understand, inform and influence foreign publics in the promotion of the national interest, and to broaden the dialogue between Americans and U.S. institutions, and their counterparts abroad[22].

---

[19] J. Wang. Telling the American story to the world: The purpose of American public diplomacy in historical perspective. In: Public Relation revue", 2007, nr. 1(33). p. 24.
[20] C. Hentea. Armele care nu ucid. Bucuresti: Nemira, 2004. p. 88.
[21] N. Cull. The Cold War and the United States Information Agency: American Propaganda and Public Diplomacy, 1945-1989. Cambridge: Cambridge University Press, 2008. 580 p.
[22] S. Miculescu. Relatii publice internationale in contextual globalizarii. Bucuresti: SNSPA, 2001. p. 60.

In the 1970s U.S. public diplomacy underwent a considerable expansion owing to the changes in the relationship between the East and the West, which fact resulted in a retuning of the rhetoric of the Cold War. All the more, a new confrontation – between the North and the South – boosted the sense of economic interdependence among the nations. The access of the large public to information and the growing importance of the human rights issue exacerbated the ongoing ideological conflict[23].

In 1982, according to the National Security Decision Directive 77 (NSDD-77) signed by president Ronald Reagan on January 14th, 1983 (declassified on January 5th, 1996), the main goal of the U.S. public diplomacy was finally formulated and still remains in full force. NSDD-77 reads that "public diplomacy includes U.S. Government public affairs activities designed to support national security objectives"[24].

Although the term 'soft power' was only developed by Joseph Nye in 1990, the 'soft power' phenomenon was attested even during the Cold War. Furthermore, that period abounds with examples showing that the United States was seeking to achieve their national interests through influence and attraction, in a bid to win the ideological battle and to export the American values (freedom, human rights, and democracy) and culture.

As mentioned above the government does not entirely control its rallying sources, especially is the case of culture because culture has no boundaries or limits. The culture is an exponent of ideas, therefore an exponent of ideology. It can infiltrate other countries and always goes hand in hand with the major conquests, by establishing a strong connection between the power and the cultural expansion, and therefore between politics and culture. Thus the persuasion through ideas can have as much impact as the persuasion by force, and even more. Culture continues to play an important role in world politics.

Cold War was mostly an ideological and psychological, was a war of images, ideas, propaganda and disinformation. In this context culture has become an important instrument for each block to persuade the largest possible number of people.

---

[23] Ch. Layne. Pacea iluzorie: marea strategie americana din 1940 pana in prezent. Iasi: Polirom, 2011. 360 p.
[24] I. D. Serban. Diplomatia publica - instrument politic pentru SUA ca smart power - analiza cauzala. In: Research and science today, 2011, nr. 1, p. 81.

14

It is interesting that both blocks East and West used the same words, like: peace, freedom, democracy but to express different realities[25]. To promote its own values, the Americans and the Soviets created, influenced and financed, either directly or indirectly, the movements, associations and magazines.

The American cultural diplomacy has the same objectives as the US public diplomacy and was based on the ideas of promoting peace and facilitating the mutual understanding between the American people and other nations. The cultural diplomacy in combination with the economic and military policies also contributed to the preservation of the U.S. strategic supremacy in Eastern Europe and minimized the communist influence in that area.

The biggest role in American cultural diplomacy plays United States identity, which is rooted in values and ideals, such as freedom, equality, democracy and human rights, mentioned in the Declaration of Independence. These ideals have shaped the political culture of the American nation and have built an exceptional image meant for the export. Such identity can be compared with the economic and military power of the United States[26].

In order to intensify the cultural exchanges between the United States and the European countries, an impressive number of institutions and programs have been created during the Cold War.

For instance, let us consider the Fulbright Program that is currently considered the most prestigious cultural, scientific and educational exchange program run by the United States worldwide. The Fulbright Program was founded by Senator J. William Fulbright from Arkansas in 1946. This program was initiated to increase mutual understanding between the people of the United States and people of other countries participating in the program through cultural and educational exchanges at the academic level.

William Fulbright proposed to offer funds both to American and foreign nationals for participating in various educational activities, such as teaching in U.S. universities, conducting researches, studying at colleges and universities. Senator

---

[25] Ch. Lepri. Du "soft power" avant l'heure: l exemple de la Guerre froid, In: Observatoire geostrategique de l'information, p. 2. 5 juillet, 2011. http://www.iris-france.org/docs/kfm_docs/docs/2011-07-12-diplomatie-publique-softpower.pdf (accessed 21.01.2012).
[26] B. Gregory. American Public Diplomacy: Enduring Characteristics, Elusive Transformation: In: Hague Journal of Diplomacy, 2011, nr. 6, p. 362.

Fulbright believed that such measure should facilitate the communication between the citizens of the United States and people of other countries[27].

Senator Fulbright's idea proved to be valid in time. Some recent research shows that 99% of the foreign graduates of the Fulbright Program mentioned that they have started "to understand better the United States and the American culture"; 96% of the graduates mentioned that they shared their American experience with their fellow citizens via the media and cultural channels after their coming back home; 89% of the respondents confirmed that their experience in the United States allowed them to take up a leading position in their country of origin[28].

At present, the United States is still acting as the world's leader in the provision of the educational services. There is a constant increase in the number of foreign students in the country. In 2014 the total number of foreign students who studied in the United States, enrolled in various programs, reached the record level of 900.000 people[29].

During the Cold War, the radio stations had a major impact on foreign audiences. The first radio station, *Voice of America*, was created by the U.S. Government, namely the *Broadcasting Board of Governors*, in 1942 during World War II. The supervising agency of the radio station was the International Broadcasting Bureau (IBB), whose declared mission was "Voice of America" – a reliable source which had to represent the entire country instead of separate segments of the American society, encompassing the American way of thinking and the activity of the United States agencies[30].

On March 15th, 1949, the U.S. government established the National Committee for a Free Europe (NCFE), and Radio Free Europe (RFE) was the branch in charge with the broadcasting in the name of the said agency. RFE was headquartered in Munich and delivered its first short-wave broadcast aimed at Czechoslovakia on July 4, 1950. The NCFE was funded by the United States Congress; the funds for RFE were allocated from the budget of the United States Central Intelligence Agency (CIA)[31].

---

[27] E.P. Panova. Vysshee obrazovanie kak potencial mjagkoj vlasti gosudarstva. B: Vestnik MGIMO-Universiteta, 2011, № 2 (15). c. 158.

[28] C. Bellamy, A. Weinberg. Educational and cultural Exchanges to restore America's image. In: The Washington Quarterly, 2008, p. 56.

[29] Record number of foreign students to enrol in 2014.
http://www.universityworldnews.com/article.php?story=2014012916402922 (accessed 16.04.14)

[30] R. Panta. Rolul diplomatiei publice in securitatea nationala a SUA. In: Studia securitatis, 2012, nr. 3. p. 38.

[31] U. Blum. Ubijstvo demokratii: operacii CRU i Pentagona v period holodnoj vojny. Moskva: Kuchkovo pole, 2013. 706 p.

The CIA played an important role in the editing activity of the central news division. In 1948, CIA created an Office of Policy Coordination (OPC) (it was merged with the CIA in 1952), which monitored the secret operations in peacetime[32].

Worldet is one of the efficient programs operated by the USIA, which became a worldwide television network connecting Washington DC with cities from 80 countries. Its representative office in Western Europe – Euronet – covered 96 local cable systems, eight televisions broadcasters and 121 hotels, hosting the TV broadcasting from Washington. Euronet broadcasts in English two hours a day, having an audience of 4 million people[33].

In the 1950s-1980s the United States public diplomacy activities were targeted primarily at the socialist countries and focused on the battle against the Soviet influence and Marxist ideology.

The fall of the Berlin Wall in 1989 pinpoints the beginning of the second stage in the history of the U.S. public diplomacy. In that period, less funding was allocated to public diplomacy, which fact resulted in its decline. After the end of the Cold War, the political leaders deemed the activity ISIA as pointless since Radio Free Europe, Hollywood and CNN were promoting successfully the United States image worldwide. In 1999 USIA was included in the State Department, losing its working format used during the Cold War.

After the events of September 11, 2001, the U.S. external policy experienced a need for restoring the public diplomacy as a means for preventing the threats posed to the national security. At the first stage of activation of public diplomacy, emphasis was placed on the application of tools whose efficiency was proven throughout the years of ideological confrontation. Those tools were supplemented with new ones in order to ensure the supremacy of the United States in the information space[34].

Richard Holbrooke, the former Assistant Secretary of State of the United States stated for Washington Post in October 2001: "Call it public diplomacy, or public affairs, or psychological warfare or – if you really want to be blunt—propaganda"[35].

The events of September 11 had a huge psychological impact. The most frequently asked question in the American society immediately after the tragic events

---

[32] R. Panta. Rolul diplomatiei publice in securitatea nationala a SUA. In: Studia securitatis, 2012, nr. 3. p. 38.
[33] G. Filimonov. "Mjagkaja sila" kul'turnoj diplomatii SShA. Moskva: RUDN, 2010. p. 118.
[34] D. Hoffman. Beyond Public Diplomacy. In: Foreign Affairs, 2002, march/april. www.foreignaffairs.com/articles/57813/david-hoffman/beyond-public-diplomacy (accessed 5.10.13).
[35] R. Holbrooke, "Get the message out," Washington Post, October 28, 2001. http://www.washingtonpost.com/wp-dyn/content/article/2010/12/13/AR2010121305410.html (accessed 5.10.2014).

was why Islamists hate the United States and what actions were to be taken in this respect in order to change their opinion[36]. The finding was that the US does not enjoy popularity in Muslim states. This is why public diplomacy activities in this period were directed to enhance the image of the United States.

At that time, such formulas were used as „war of ideas" or „struggle for people's hearts and minds"[37]. These formulations persist until today. Citing the *United States National Security Strategy of 2002*, Bruce Gregory stated that an efficient public diplomacy can only help the people of the United States win a war of ideas, such as the war on international terrorism[38].

The administration of George Bush Jr. pinpointed the seven pillars of the United Stated public diplomacy[39]. The foundation of the public diplomacy rests on the political component, which reads that the foreign public should understand the United States politics as it is, that is, not as commented by politicians, media etc.

The United States government prefers offering their own account of the events, by publishing information in a lot of foreign newspapers or by broadcasting them on TV and radio. Thus the United States government is seeking to explain the United States politics by making reference to the universal values and the American cultures[40].

It is crucial for the conveyed message to be credible and authentic. Broadcasting the message is not enough; it should also be tailored to the specific audiences, after the target group and its possible reaction to the public diplomacy program have been considered[41].

The Office of Public Affairs played a special part in the organization of public diplomacy activities during the Bush administration. This agency was a structure of the United States Department of State whose purposes were to enhance the United States image and to explain their political objectives both on domestic and external scales[42]. To prevent disinformation, White House had a Department of Audiovisual

---

[36] R. Panta. Rolul diplomatiei publice in securitatea nationala a SUA. In: Studia securitatis, 2012, nr. 3. p. 39.
[37] Ed. Djerejian. Changing Minds, Winning Peace: A New Strategic Direction for U.S. Public Diplomacy in the Arab & Muslin World. http://www.state.gov/documents/ organization/24882.pdf (accessed 14.08.12).
[38] B. Gregory. Public Diplomacy and National Security: Lessons from the U.S. Experience. http://smallwarsjournal.com/jrnl/art/public-diplomacy-and-national-security. (accessed 5.11.13)
[39] Ch. Ross Pillars of Public Diplomacy. In: Harvard International Review, 2006. http://hir.harvard.edu/china/pillars-of-public-diplomacy (accessed 12.12.12)
[40] R. Panta. Rolul diplomatiei publice in securitatea nationala a SUA. In: Studia securitatis, 2012, nr. 3. p. 39.
[41] Ch. Ross Pillars of Public Diplomacy. In: Harvard International Review, 2006. http://hir.harvard.edu/china/pillars-of-public-diplomacy (accessed 12.12.12)
[42] About the Office of Public Affairs. http://www.dhs.gov/about-office-public-affairs (accessed 04.02.15)

comprising a number of information centers that sought to put into practice specific actions of public diplomacy in due time.

In 2002 an information campaign on the United States was conducted under the leadership of Under Secretary for Public Diplomacy and Public Affairs Charlotte Beers. The United States intensified sharply external communication initially in regard to Arab States and later in regard to the areas where Islam is the prevailing religion[43].

In 2001-2002, were allocated significant funds for public diplomacy activity but without considerable success. Against a background of ongoing eradication of Anti-Americanism through U.S. public diplomacy programs, the anti-American sentiment persisted and emanated from the mistrust of the United States politics, leaders and political institutions[44]. There are some explanations.

1. Public diplomacy activities took up the public diplomacy paradigm used during the Cold War, which only implied convincing people and therefore did not prove to be effective.

2. After a period of low funding of public diplomacy, the Bush administration would raise the funding of that field, so that in 2007 the amount allocated for public diplomacy activities was of 351 million USD[45], an insufficient amount yet, which makes up 0.75% of the U.S. military budget.

3. United States did not have a normative basis for new public diplomacy strategy.

United States under Secretary for Public Diplomacy and Public Affairs in 2005-2007, Karen Hughes, mentioned that following the events of 11 September 2001, the dialogue between the United States and the rest of the world has been based on the following strategic principles:

1. Offering a positive vision, hope, as well as possibilities for people around the world; such vision is rooted in a sustainable commitment to freedom;

2. Isolating and marginalizing the violent extremists and undermining their efforts aimed at exploiting religion as a tool for rationalizing their acts of terror.

3. Favoring a community of interests and values shared by people from the United States and many other countries[46].

---

[43] A. Dolinskij, Diskurs o publichnoj diplomatii. In: Mezhdunarodnye processy", 2011, nr. 3. http://www.intertrends.ru/twenty-fifth/008.htm (accessed 04.02.15)
[44] R. Panta. Rolul diplomatiei publice in securitatea nationala a SUA. In: Studia securitatis, 2012, nr. 3. p. 40.
[45] S.M. Samujlov. "Diplomatija preobrazovanij" Kondolizy Rajs i reformirovanie Gosdepartamenta SShA. B: Jekonomika, politika, kul'tura, 2008, Janvar'. No. 1. c. 30.
[46] R. S. Zaharna. The network paradigm of Strategic Public Diplomacy. In: Policy Brief, 2005, vol 10, nr.1 april 2005. https://www.american.edu/soc/faculty/upload/Network-Paradigm.pdf (accessed 12.04.13)

In the course of her mandate, Karen Hughes intensified the public diplomacy activities, particularly by opening information centers in London, Dubai and Brussels. The American electronic resources oriented towards Europe and Near East increased in that period. The United States Department of State gave a positive appraisal of those centers as they ensured the broadcasting of their participation in TV and radio broadcasts, either news or shows, in Europe and Near East"[47].

After 2002, the U.S. Department of State assisted by the communication experts of the U.S. government began exploring the potential of the new Internet-based social media, in a bid to win the hearts and minds of the citizens of other countries, particularly of Muslim countries that were plunged in the war of ideas. The finding was unanimous –"the age of mass information, everyone – starting with political candidates and ending with terrorists – is to interact instantly and permanently with the public"[48].

Reaching such conclusion, a number of experts as well as many representatives of the executive and legislative authorities of the United States have recognized the importance of public diplomacy. Therefore, they have come to believe that public diplomacy should be put in place in order to create a favorable atmosphere abroad and thus to contribute to the success of the political, military and economic actions of the United States.

During this period, important documents were developed for US public diplomacy. In 2007 the American Center for Strategic and International Studies released the report *A Smarter, More Secure America*, which is an attempt of adapting the concept of 'smart power' to the American reality.

A commission had been set up before the release of the report *A Smarter, More Secure America* for the purpose of applying the concept of 'smart power' to the American reality. Richard L. Armitage and Joseph S. Nye, in their capacity of members of that commission, have come to the conclusion that keeping the status of a superpower of the United States implies changing its foreign policy strategy. The new strategy must rest upon the following five elements: the alliances and the collaboration with other countries via various international institutions, global development, public diplomacy, economic integration, and technology and

---

[47]S.M. Samujlov. "Diplomatija preobrazovanij" Kondolizy Rajs i reformirovanie Gosdepartamenta SShA. B: Jekonomika, politika, kul'tura, 2008, Janvar'. No. 1. c. 30.
[48] Al- Cl. Rata. Aplicatii ale internetului și noua diplomatie digitala. In: Cultura și comunicare, 2011, nr. 5. p. 2 http://culturasicomunicare.com/pdf/2011/Rata%20Alex.pdf (accessed 25.12.2013)

innovation. The commission decided that the very tool for putting into practice the concept of 'smart power' in the context of the American reality was public diplomacy[49].

The analysis of the American public diplomacy activities in the early 21st century, along with the evolution of the academic speech in this regard, oriented public diplomacy towards cooperation[50]. United States under Secretary for Public Diplomacy and Public Affairs Karen Hughes, in 2005, called it "a new paradigm", considering the fact that changing the objectives of external communication in a completely re-shaped context requires new principles of thinking[51].

Following its creation in 2006, the Interministerial Coordinating Committee for Public Diplomacy and Strategic Communication launched a new strategy for public diplomacy in 2007, which mentioned that the priority of U.S. public diplomacy was to expand the educational and exchange programs[52].

Setting an indispensable connection between the strategic communication and public diplomacy, the Policy Coordinating Committee released the *U.S. National Strategy for Public Diplomacy and Strategic Communication* in 2007. That official document reads that the strength, success and security of the United States of America rest on its commitment to certain values and principles that govern its actions in the world through public diplomacy. In particular, the latter is important for activities, such as advocating freedom, human rights, dignity and equality, etc.

As stated in the *U.S. National Strategy for Public Diplomacy and Strategic Communication*, the objectives governing America's public diplomacy include, in the first place, offering a positive vision of hope and opportunity of the United States as a country where it is considered that all people deserve to live in just societies that are governed by the rule of law and free from corruption and intimidation; where it is considered that people should be able to speak their minds, protest peacefully, work

---

[49] R. Panta. Rolul diplomatiei publice in securitatea nationala a SUA. In: Studia securitatis, 2012, nr. 3. p. 41.
[50] A. Dolinskij, Diskurs o publichnoj diplomatii. In: Mezhdunarodnye processy", 2011, nr. 3. http://www.intertrends.ru/twenty-fifth/008.htm (accessed 04.02.15)
[51] K. Hughes"Waging Peace": A New Paradigm for Public Diplomacy. In: Mediterranean Quarterly", 2007, p. 18-37.
[52] U.S. National Strategy for Public Diplomacy and Strategic Communication. Strategic Communication and Public Diplomacy Policy Coordinating Committee (PCC). June 2007. http://www.au.af.mil/au/awc/awcgate/state/natstrat_strat_comm.pdf. (accessed 04.02.14)

and participate in choosing their government, be educated in order to become responsible and tolerant citizens in a world of prosperity[53] .

The second objective emphasizes the collaboration with the partners and the effort for isolating and marginalizing violent extremists who threaten the freedom and peace. This objective can be achieved by promoting democratization as a path to a positive future, engaging Muslim communities, isolating and discrediting terrorist leaders, de-legitimizing terror as a tactic to achieve political ends, demonstrating that the West is open to all religions and is not in conflict with any faith[54].

The last objective refers to the nurture of common values and interests between American and peoples of other countries, cultures and faiths across the world[55]. In addition, the document under consideration determines the strategic audiences addressed by U.S. public diplomacy.

The first category includes the key influencers, such as clerics, journalists, women leaders, business and labor leaders, political leaders, scientists and military personnel. The second category covers those groups that are most vulnerable to extremist ideology, that is, youth, women and girls, and minorities. The third category refers to mass audiences. The priorities of public diplomacy consist in expanding education and exchange programs, modernizing communication etc[56].

In the *Strategic Communications and Countering Ideological Support for Terrorism* released in 2007, public diplomacy is regarded as an extremely important factor. Such position is sustained with the tools that had been efficient during the Cold War, such as educational exchanges, publications and information broadcast via media, which were intended to make known to everyone the American values, democracy, freedom of expression / religion / markets.

However, considering the present-day security environment, which has changed completely, these tools are not sufficient any longer. To become efficient in terms of national security, public diplomacy needs to have its activities combined with an effective partnership with the agencies that carry out activities of public diplomacy,

---

[53] U.S. National Strategy for Public Diplomacy and Strategic Communication. Strategic Communication and Public Diplomacy Policy Coordinating Committee (PCC). June 2007.
p. 3 http://www.au.af.mil/au/awc/awcgate/state/natstrat_strat_comm.pdf. (accessed 04.02.2014)
[54] U.S. National Strategy for Public Diplomacy and Strategic Communication. Strategic Communication and Public Diplomacy Policy Coordinating Committee (PCC). June 2007.
p. 3 http://www.au.af.mil/au/awc/awcgate/state/natstrat_strat_comm.pdf. (accessed 04.02.2014)
[55] I. D. Serban. Diplomatia publica - instrument politic pentru SUA ca smart power - analiza cauzala. in: Research and science today, 2011, nr. 1, p. 79-91.
[56] R. Panta. Rolul diplomatiei publice in securitatea nationala a SUA. In: Studia securitatis, 2012, nr. 3. p. 42.

supervise the virtual environment and terrorist propaganda via the Arabic websites, which means turning into *a new United States public diplomacy*. The new public diplomacy is directly influenced by the public policy. Therefore, in the opinion of Bruce Gregory, it is the tools that have already proven to be efficient that should be applied, such as adjusting the message to the target audience, outlining the nuances and explaining the threats, actively involving the civil society in the citizen-government dialogue, ensuring more flexible public diplomacy structures and actions, and involving the media and Internet[57].

Before the arrival of the Internet, U.S. public diplomacy had been implemented via the radio and television. The ever-growing audience listening to radio broadcasts, watching TV shows on the Internet and discussing the major social and political issues on social networks has changed the nature of contemporary public diplomacy, as the target audience currently includes millions of citizens using 600.000 social networks[58].

There are a number of terms used to express the innovative ways of influencing the audience via the Internet, such as digital diplomacy, online diplomacy (Internet diplomacy), diplomacy social networks (Twitter diplomacy) and *Web 2.0 public diplomacy*. Russian researcher N. A. Cvetkova considers that the most frequent term used by the American political leaders is the last-mentioned one. In the United States *Web 2.0 public diplomacy* software is developed by corporations specializing in Internet-related services and products, with Google Corporation being one of the market leaders[59].

American online magazines have a major influence on young people, who are kept informed through visual images and videos. In the meantime, while monitoring the social networks, Washington can guide the discussions of the bloggers in the right direction. The personal web pages of the political representatives on such social networks as Facebook and Twitter facilitate the communication between Washington and the social networks users. Finally, SMS sending on mobile telephones makes it

---

[57] B. Gregory . Public Diplomacy and National Security: Lessons from the U.S. Experience. In: Small Wars Journal, 2008, august. www.smallwarsjournal.com (accessed 11.06.2013).
[58] N.A. Cvetkova. Programmy web 2.0. v publichnoj diplomatii SShA. B: SShA i Kanada: Jekonomika, politika, kul'tura, 2011, no. 3, p. 110.
[59] E. Zinov'eva. Cifrovaja diplomatija, mezhdunarodnaja bezopasnost' i vozmozhnosti dlja Rossii. B: SShA i Kanada: Jekonomika, politika, kul'tura, 2011, no. 3, p. 213-228.

possible for the U.S. government to have access to people who do not use the Internet[60].

The Internet started to be used as a public diplomacy tool in the United States at the initiative of Head of the United States Information Agency John Duffy in 1996[61]. He merged several magazines which had lost relevance as the ideological confrontation with the Soviet Union came to an end. In this way, John Duffy created the first online magazine – *The Washington File.*

The emergence of a new political and ideological enemy of the United States, that is, the Islamic fundamentalism, was a strong impulse for using the web as an external policy tool. In 2002-2003 the Bush administration transferred the radio and television on the Internet. In the same time, several TV channels were launched to reach foreign audience. In 2006 was set up the first team to monitor the information about the United States that was circulating through social networks. In the same year the U.S. Department of State official blog *DipNote* was launched. The Bush administration opened the portal *America.gov* that displays information about the United States and some online magazines (*eJournal USA, Weekly News Bulletin, CornerStudent* etc.)[62]. These sites play an important role in American public diplomacy.

Reforms in public diplomacy initiated by the administration Bush Jr. were continued by the Obama administration. When coming to office in 2009, President Barack Obama announced the new standards of U.S. public diplomacy inspired from *U.S. Public Diplomacy: Background and Current Issues*[63].

The initiatives of the Obama administration in the field of public diplomacy are based on the following findings: the disastrous image of the United States, particularly in the Arab and Muslim world; the growing power of the civil society; the opinion globalization and unprecedented development of new Internet-related technologies. It should also be noted that there are some factors that cause the classical public diplomacy to fall behind the new means of communications[64].

The Internet and social networks are currently considered diplomatic tools used for a dual purpose: they support the employment policy implemented by the United

---

[60] N.A. Cvetkova. Programmy web 2.0. v publichnoj diplomatii SShA. B: SShA i Kanada: Jekonomika, politika, kul'tura, 2011, no. 3, p. 113.

[61] V.V. Lukov. Internet kak instrument politicheskih tehnologij v SShA. B: SShA i Kanada: Jekonomika, politika, kul'tura, 2005, no. 5, c. 96.

[62] V.V. Lukov. Internet kak instrument politicheskih tehnologij v SShA. B: SShA i Kanada: Jekonomika, politika, kul'tura, 2005, no. 5, c. 98.

[63] K. H. Nakamura, M. C Weed. U.S. Public Diplomacy: Background and Current Issues, Congressional Research Service. www.crs.gov. (accessed 18.12.13)

[64] J. Nocetti. La diplomatie d'Obama à l'épreuve du Web 2.0. In: Politique étrangère, 2011, nr. 1, p. 157.

States government and accompany the democratization of the countries that maintain complex relationships with the United States[65]. Considering the current international background, which is characterized with the growth of the influence exerted by the civil society and new technologies, the freedom of the Internet, is one of the central guidelines of the external policy of the Obama administration[66].

Extension of American democracy continues to be a feature of US public diplomacy. In the context of globalization, the democratization is also through communication technologies.

The organization *21st Century Statecraft* was created to support and train cyber-dissidents abroad in the name of the information flow freedom and human rights. Thus, *Civil Society 2.0* was launched as part of *21st Century Statecraft* in 2009 for the purpose of identifying the dissidents' worldwide and supplying digital technologies to them[67].

In her speech delivered in Washington on February 15th 2011, Hillary Clinton mentioned that connection technologies are accelerants of political, social, and economic change. She also stated that the U.S. government allocated 20 million Euros for the up keeping of the tools that stimulate the freedom of expression on the Internet[68].

Following her appointment to office, Hillary Clinton launched several initiatives transforming the Internet into an important element of the U.S. external policy. At a lecture delivered at the New York University, Clinton presented the outlines of the program *How to govern in the 21st Century*. She announced that the freedom given by the Internet would be, since that moment, a key component of the U.S. diplomacy[69].

The document *IT Strategic Plan: Fiscal Years 2011-2013 – Digital Diplomacy* contains a specification of the digital diplomacy directions in terms of implementation of the U.S. external policy priorities. In particular, those priorities included *inter alia* achieving international security and offering a positive vision

---

[65] J. Nocetti. La diplomatie d'Obama à l'épreuve du Web 2.0. In: Politique étrangère, 2011, nr. 1, p. 157.

[66] N. Arpagian Washington apporte son soutien technique aux cyberdissidents. In: Observatoire géostratégique de l'information. Diplomatie publique, soft power...influence d'état", 2011, 5 juillet. p. 6 http://www.iris-france.org/docs/kfm_docs/docs/2011-07-12-diplomatie-publique-softpower.pdf. (accessed 28.04.12)

[67] R. Panta. Rolul diplomatiei publice in securitatea nationala a SUA. In: Studia securitatis, 2012, nr. 3. p. 44.

[68] N. Arpagian. Washington apporte son soutien technique aux cyberdissidents. In: Observatoire géostratégique de l'information. Diplomatie publique, soft power...influence d'état", 2011, 5 juillet. p. 6. http://www.iris-france.org/docs/kfm_docs/docs/2011-07-12-diplomatie-publique-softpower.pdf. (accessed 28.04.12)

[69] J. Nocetti. La diplomatie d'Obama à l'épreuve du Web 2.0. In: Politique étrangère, 2011, nr. 1, p. 157.

abroad. Digital diplomacy was expected to be implemented in the following directions: funding projects for the development and dissemination of new technologies allowing ruling out censorship; creating information agencies to support the opposition in the authoritarian regimes; creating an underground Internet and independent mobile telephony networks in third countries to allow fighters against authoritarian regimes to exchange information online[70].

In the same time, the U.S. adopted documents concerning the political and military aspects of Internet development. In June 2010 the *U.S. Department of Defense Strategy for Operating in Cyberspace* was published. That document read that the cyberspace was a battle space, just as the land, maritime and air space.

The Pentagon's strategy developed the concept of U.S. national security of 2010, which was based on the assertion that the cyberspace was a battlefield[71]. When analyzing the U.S. policy in this field, the Russian expert E.A. Rogovski mentioned that the end point of this type of diplomacy was the acknowledgement of the U.S. status of world leader[72].

In 2011 the U.S. *Web 2.0 public diplomacy* came into sharp focus on a worldwide scale in the context of the ongoing Arabic Spring, as it burst into waves of protests in the Near East and Northern Africa, called *twitter revolutions* by the journalists. It is considered that the social networks acted as a catalyzer in the middle of those events, while the key reasons were the social, economic and political conditions in those countries[73].

In conclusion, we can state that U.S. public diplomacy was primarily an external policy tool to fulfill the needs in the inter-war period of the 20th century. The mission of the two agencies – U.S. Committee on Public Information and U.S. Office of War Information – was to contribute to the victory of the United States by disseminating information.

Secondly, U.S. public diplomacy plays an important part in the propagation of the democratic values around the globe. The USIA, which coordinated the public

---

[70]E. Chernenko. Internet - protokol'naja sluzhba Gosdepa. B: Kommersant, 2011, 15 sentjabrja, http://www.kommersant.ru/doc-rss/1773567 (accessed 31.08.2012).
[71]National Security Strategy, may 2010. p. 27.
http://www.whitehouse.gov/sites/default/files/rss_viewer/national_security_strategy.pdf (accessed 21.03.14)
[72]E. Rogovskij SShA: informacionnoe obshhestvo. Jekonomika i politika. Moskva: Mezhdunarod¬nye otnoshenija, 2008. c. 354.
[73]O. Demidov. Social'nye setevye servisy v kontekste mezhdunarodnoj i nacional'noj bezopasnosti. B: Indeks bezopasnosti, 2013, Vesna, nr. 1 (104), c. 65 -76.

diplomacy activities during the Cold War, had the mission to understand, inform and influence foreign publics in promotion of the national interest, and to broaden the dialogue between Americans and U.S. institutions, and their counterparts abroad.

Thirdly, following September 11th 2001, the aim of U.S. public diplomacy was not only to promote the American policies and values, but mainly to facilitate their understanding through adaptation to the foreign public and by favoring a community of interests and values shared by people from the United States and many other countries.

At present the United States is applying both the public diplomacy tools used during the Cold War (cultural and educational exchange, media, political statements etc.), as well as new tools in order to ensure the U.S. supremacy in the information space. The Internet freedom is one of the cornerstones of the external policy carried out by the Obama administration.

Other specific features of the new American strategy in the field of external policy are as follows: alliances and partnership with other countries via various international institutions, global development, public diplomacy, economic integration, and technology and innovation. The American power, success and national security depend on the principles and values applied by the U.S. in the external policy via public diplomacy.

The development of public diplomacy after September 11th 2001 confirms the importance of this national security tool for the United States. Although no remarkable results have been noted in the first decade of the 21st century, the success of the Obama administration in this regard proves that public diplomacy will keep having an impact on the American way of formulating and implementing the policies and strategies of foreign policy and national security.

3. The role of soft power in China's public diplomacy

China's economic rise in the last 20 years has ranked it undeniably among the key players at a global scale. That rise entailed some uncertainties in regard to such issues as overturning strategic balances, redefining economic rules, questioning the democratic system as the unique system able to achieve prosperity and, implicitly, the emergence of a new military power[74].

China holds all the advantages of a great power. It is an nuclear, demographic and economic power. China has natural riches and keeps developing its military capacities. Its permanent membership in the UN Security Council allows China to put political pressure on all the players at the worldwide level.

Having started in the 1990s, China's extraordinary economic growth opened the way for the globalization that has become an 'instrument' for conquering the international arena[75].

The adherence to the World Trade Organization (WTO) in 2001 marked the launch of the strategy, which made it possible for China to extend both its access to global markets and its exporting / importing capacities. China keeps promoting an active policy on the international stage in order to fulfill the needs for market expansion and diversification.

At the same time, China has adopted a diplomatic strategy, as well as a strategy of massive investments in a bid to secure Beijing's access to the channels of supply and turnover of goods and energy resources[76].

The rapid economic expansion has provided China with resources for putting in place an active diplomacy having an increasing political influence on a worldwide scale. Following the 1990s and the events in Tiananmen, China engaged in the way out of the diplomatic isolation where it used to be and changed its attitude towards the international community[77].

In the analysis of Chinese public diplomacy is important to mention three elements which exert a great influence and explain the specifics of Chinese public diplomacy:

1. the traditional scrupulosity in upholding the country image,

---

[74]R.Megali Puissance Chine. La stratégie d'affirmation internationale chinoise. www.defense.gouv.fr/irsem/publications/fiches/fiches-de-l-irsem. (accessed 12.03.13)
[75] R. Panta. Rolul „soft power" in diplomatia publica chineza. In: Studia securitatis, 2013, nr. 1. p. 64.
[76]R.Megali. Puissance Chine. La stratégie d'affirmation internationale chinoise. www.defense.gouv.fr/irsem/publications/fiches/fiches-de-l-irsem. (accessed 12.03.13)
[77] Ph. Le Corre. La Chine, nouvel acteur des relations internationales. In: Etudes, 2006, nr. 10, p. 310.

2. the history of the external propaganda practiced by the communist regime.

3. the awareness of the key role to be played by public diplomacy and communication in the contemporary world[78].

In accordance with the first element, the Chinese are very sensitive to the way the foreigners perceive China (and the Chinese external policy). This fact ensures a connection with the 'image' of China, which is crucial though difficult to understand by the Westerners.

One of historiography problems of Chinese public diplomacy is to establish when China began to use elements of public diplomacy. The American political scientist Andrew Scobell considers that the imperial China used its culture as a source of legitimacy and hegemonic power within a system based on tribute, and invited the foreign public officials to make pilgrimages to China[79]. The Chinese leaders always knew how to please their guests. Such hegemonic system, founded on soft power, ceased to exist in the second half of the 19th century on the background of China's relative decline and transformation into a semi-colony of Japan and Western powers.

Laurent Hou and Matthias Kaufman believe that the Republic of China has been using public diplomacy to achieve economic and political goals even since the Cold War[80]. The Maoist China was the non-official mentor of the non-alignment movement that dates back to the conference of Bandung in 1955, and used propaganda to promote its revolutionary and development model among other third world countries[81].

Most of the researchers who analyzed the Chinese public diplomacy consider that in the early 1970s China discovered the cultural public diplomacy techniques. For example, in 1971 China sent an invitation to the American tennis team to come in China. Purpose of this invitation was the rapprochement between the Chinese and United States governments.

---

[78] N. Cull. China's Propaganda and Influence Operations, its Intelligence Activities that Target the United States and its Resulting Impacts on US National Security. Testimony before the US-China. In: Economic and Security Review Commission Hearing", 30 April 2009, disponibil pe http://www.uscc.gov/hearings/2009hearings/transcripts/09_04_30_trans/09_04_30_trans.pdf (accessed 24. 06. 2012)

[79] A. Scobell. China's soft sell: Is the world buying? In: China Brief Volume. http://www.jamestown.org. (accessed 28.04.12)

[80] L. Hou, M. Kaufmann. Séduire l'Europe: la diplomatie publique chinoise en action, partie 2. La fin et les moyens, 2011. http://www.china-institute.org/articles/Seduire_l_Europe_la_diplomatie_publique_chinoise_en_action2. (accessed 12.05.2012)

[81] G. D. Rawnsley. China Talks Back – Public Diplomacy and Soft Power for the Chinese Century. In: Handbook of Public Diplomacy. New-York: Routledge, 2009, p. 285.

Also, Mao Zedong made use of the ping-pong diplomacy when he had recourse to panda diplomacy in the relationship with London and Washington by re-activating a centuries-old practice of offering panda bears, which are considered China's symbolic ambassadors[82].

In the period of years 1978-2000 the reforms undertaken by Deng Hiaoping – the architect of the Chinese economy – boosted the expansion of China's public diplomacy. It was for the first time that the Ministry of Foreign Affairs of the People's Republic of China appointed a spokesperson in 1984 and began to hold press conferences on a regular basis[83].

The second element of Chinese public diplomacy - the history of the external propaganda practiced by the communist regime is closely linked with the demonstrations on Tiananmen Square in 1989.

These events mark a turning point in the evolution of Chinese public diplomacy[84] and represented both a crisis within the Chinese political system and China's negative international image. The Tiananmen Square massacre was the most atrocious event of China's contemporary history.

After this event, the Chinese propaganda has been working hard to *re-build China's international image*, using new technologies and methodologies and also keeping elements from the past. China also began to use public diplomacy *to promote its image*.

In China most of the definitions read that all the messages aiming to influence other people are propagandistic. Most experts consider that the concept of 'propaganda' can be used to characterize China's public communication ever since the creation of the People's Republic until late in the 1980s – a period when the Chinese government was disseminating mainly distorted information.

Prior to the policy of openness advocated by Deng, the purpose of the China's public diplomacy was to create a positive image of an autarchic state. Since the late 1970s, the purpose of China's public diplomacy was shifted to the legitimation of the communist power. Such mission was supplemented by the need for attracting foreign investments and redressing China's negative image.

The Chinese leaders have come to understand that the efforts made in the field of public diplomacy need to be followed by credible actions, in order to achieve a

---

[82] G. D. Rawnsley, China Talks Back – Public Diplomacy and Soft Power for the Chinese Century. In: Handbook of Public Diplomacy. New-York: Routledge, 2009, p. 285.
[83] R. Panta Rolul „soft power" in diplomatia publica chineza. In: Studia securitatis, 2013, nr. 1. p. 67.
[84] R. Panta Rolul „soft power" in diplomatia publica chineza. In: Studia securitatis, 2013, nr. 1. p. 68.

successful communication[85]. Such attitude could be explained by the need to convince and attract economic partners. In order to fulfill such goals, China's government contracted the services of the public relations company Hill & Knowlton[86].

China's public diplomacy is of particular interest due to some two factors.

Firstly, China is a single-party country having a centralized authoritarian regime that holds the control of its public diplomacy. Therefore, it appears that China can build upon a tradition of political propaganda. Generally speaking, this country carries out a state-centered diplomacy, which is specific to the period of the Cold War.

Secondly, the Chinese leaders have come to understand that the legitimacy of their regime – both internally and externally – depends on its economic growth [87].

China's public diplomacy aims at achieving three objectives:

1. "China is a country working to offer its people a better future and seeking ways for its political system to be better understood";

2. "China is willing to be regarded as a stable, responsible and trustworthy economic partner" and aspires to be seen as a prospective economic power, whose development does not arouse fear. Such objective relates to the external policy and the strategy of 'good neighborliness'.

3. "The Chinese leaders are willing to be considered as being responsible and trustworthy by the members of the international community"[88].

Ten years after the events of Tiananmen – China's public diplomacy gained momentum and more professionalism.

Application of the concept of soft power at the Chinese reality

'Soft power' was re-fined after 2000 by the Chinese intellectuals and adjusted to the Chinese strategic imperatives. Soft power (*ruan quanli*) was publicly declared as the official strategy of China's external policy at the 27th congress of the Communist

---

[85] I. D'Hooghe. The Rise of China's Public Diplomacy. In: Clingendael Diplomacy Papers, 2007, nr. 12, p. 21. http://www.clingendael.nl/publications/2007/20070700_cdsp_paper_hooghe.pdf (accessed 28.04.12)

[86] P. André. La notion d'état dans la pensée politique chinoise et ses conséquences sur la scène internationale. p. 453. http://www.youscribe.com/catalogue/rapports-et-theses/savoirs/sciences-humaines-et-sociales/la-notion-d-etat-dans-la-pensee-politique-chinoise-et-ses-1524848 (accessed 28.04.12).

[87] P. André. La notion d'état dans la pensée politique chinoise et ses conséquences sur la scène internationale. p. 452. http://www.youscribe.com/catalogue/rapports-et-theses/savoirs/sciences-humaines-et-sociales/la-notion-d-etat-dans-la-pensee-politique-chinoise-et-ses-1524848 (accessed 28.04.12).

[88] I. D'Hooghe The Rise of China's Public Diplomacy. In: Clingendael Diplomacy Papers, 2007, nr. 12, p. 18-19. http://www.clingendael.nl/publications/2007/20070700_cdsp_paper_hooghe.pdf (accessed 28.04.12)

Party of the People's Republic of China in October 2007[89]. There are several tools of such strategy like the Chinese culture, the history of one of the oldest civilizations, the subtle Chinese arts and calligraphy. B. Courmont mentions cultural advantages and the manner in which these soft power tools are used within a global strategy[90].

Chinese intellectuals and politicians also consider the Chinese cultural a factor of differentiation and at the same time an asset for the Chinese soft power. An important role in this concept it had an article published in China in 1993. Its author Wang Huning identified the culture as the main source of the Chinese soft power. Since then, all the academic discourses have evolved around this central idea, while the phrase 'cultural soft power' is often used in the formal Chinese language[91]. Chinese culture is the heart of public diplomacy and cultural soft power development is essential for the consolidation of China's international status.

Beijing made the culture its main strategy of the public diplomacy for the entire world. The Chinese public diplomacy uses the culture as a strategic 'instrument'. The Chinese president Hu Jintao mentioned that the Chinese nation would grow, without any doubt, through the prosperity of culture[92]. China uses this non-politic element as an important vector to extend its influence in the world. This strategy addresses to nations which have a negative opinion about the Chinese government, but also to avoid the diplomatic tensions in topics as: Tibet and press freedom.

Despite the Chinese public diplomacy efforts, China's image in Europe has been spoiled the recent years. According to a survey conducted by Pew Research Center, the percentage of the population which has a positive global vision about China, decreases from 65% in 2005 and 47% in 2008 in Great Britain, from 58% to 28% in France and from 46% to 26% in Germany[93]. This research revealed that the Europeans are skeptical concerning the Chinese political values and principles.

---

[89]M. Bassan Le soft-power chinois en Afrique. In: Fiche de l'Irsem", 2012, nr. 13, p. 3. http://www.irsem.defense.gouv.fr (accessed 18.05.13).

[90] B. Courmont. Chine, la grande séduction: essai sur le soft power chinois. Paris: Choiseul, 2009. http://www.diploweb.com/Chine-La-grande-seduction-Essai.html (accessed 28.04.12)

[91]M. Bassan Le soft-power chinois en Afrique. In: Fiche de l'Irsem", 2012, nr. 13, p. 3. http://www.irsem.defense.gouv.fr (accessed 18.05.13)

[92]L. Hou, M. Kaufmann Séduire l'Europe: la diplomatie publique chinoise en action. partie 3. La stratégie chinoise porte-t-elle ses fruits?,
http://www.china-institute.org/articles/Seduire_1_Europe_la_diplomatie_publique_chinoise_en_action3.
(accessed 28.04.12)

[93] L. Hou, M. Kaufmann. Séduire l'Europe: la diplomatie publique chinoise en action. partie 3. La stratégie chinoise porte-t-elle ses fruits?, p. 2
http://www.china-institute.org/articles/Seduire_1_Europe_la_diplomatie_publique_chinoise_en_action3.
(accessed 28.04.12)

Another survey realized by BBC World Service shows at the beginning of 2009, that the Olympic Games didn't ameliorate China's image, within the citizens of the three European powers. From a Chinese perspective, this lack of affection of the European audience is due to a fundamental misunderstanding, which is maintained by media and accustomed in absence of knowledge on Chinese specific circumstances and politics.

To remediate this situation, Zhao Qizheng, the vice-director of the Foreign Affairs Committee within the Central Committee of the Chinese Communist Party, proposed, in March 2010, to organize an imposing public diplomacy campaign. The main obstacle to realize this campaign was the incompatibility of the used messages and methods. Even if the Chinese public diplomacy evolved long after the Maoist age, it remains very close to propaganda. It is a huge contrast between the messages of 'harmony' and 'peace' and the reality of an authoritarian regime, which suppress the public opposition, and cancel the influence of the Chinese public diplomacy in Europe.

Although the Chinese government hasn't decided yet if the public diplomacy would exclusively depend on the state actors[94] the State Council Information Office is the supreme authority of the Chinese public diplomacy.

At the end of 1991, during the National Conference of the 'external propaganda', was created the State Council Foreign Propaganda Office. Nowadays Beijing prefers to name it the State Council External Publicity Office. Until then the organization of propaganda and official communication were assigned to the Bureau of Propaganda of the Chinese Communist Party. Organizationally, this institution confirms the separation between the state structure and the communist party structure. The Council's purpose is to promote China as a stable state in process of reform, a state which takes care of its population, inclusive the national minorities fighting against poverty[95].

The Chinese leaders consider that the country's negative image is a consequence of the lack of knowledge or misunderstanding of the Chinese values and culture.

---

[94] L. Hou, M. Kaufmann Séduire l'Europe: la diplomatie publique chinoise en action. partie 3. La stratégie chinoise porte-t-elle ses fruits?, p. 8.
http://www.china-institute.org/articles/Seduire_1_Europe_la_diplomatie_publique_chinoise_en_action3. (accessed 28.04.12)
[95] P. André. La notion d'état dans la pensée politique chinoise et ses conséquences sur la scène internationale. p. 455. http://www.youscribe.com/catalogue/rapports-et-theses/savoirs/sciences-humaines-et-sociales/la-notion-d-etat-dans-la-pensee-politique-chinoise-et-ses-1524848 (accessed 28.04.12)

They are convinced that by learning the language and culture of this country, can be promoted the image of China. As a result, the last few years Beijing invested in promoting the Chinese art and language in almost all the Europeans states through film, cultural events, studying the Chinese language.

Most of the conceptions used by China to promote its image abroad are based on consensual and shareable values, such as *'harmony'* or *'peace'*. On the other hand, the Western countries' discourse is focused on the protection of human rights and a rich universally-oriented conceptual basis.

At the plenary session of the 2003, Boao Forum for Asia, Zheng Bijan from the Propaganda Department proposed to use the concept of 'peaceful rise' (*hepning jueqi*) as one the key concepts of China's public diplomacy.

This concept was re-used in 2005 White Book and re-phrased as 'peaceful development' (*heping fazhan*) on account of some terminological issue. The moderate politicians criticized the term 'rise', while the representatives of People's Liberation Army did not accept the use of the adjective 'peaceful'. Currently, the terms 'peaceful development' and 'peaceful development road' are most frequently used as 'development' is an economic concept, while the concept of 'rise' implies the ascension of China's influence in the international relations[96].

In October 2007, the President of China Hu Jintao stated that China's economic development depended on the construction and maintenance of a stable regional environment, and the concept of 'peaceful development' explained the decision of adapting the traditional views of Confucius to the reality, such as seeking harmony, union without uniformity, promoting cooperation both in the Chinese society and at a worldwide level[97].

The *peaceful development* represents the cornerstone of China's public diplomacy. In the opinion of Professor Wu Jianmin, 'peaceful development' implies three negations: no expansion (denial of colonial power road), no hegemony and no alliances with one or several powers, so as to avoid a new Cold War[98].

The concept of 'peaceful rise' mainly refers to East Asian countries (a region which bewares China's development, yet being an important area due to the raw materials supplied to China's economy.

---

[96] R. Panta. Rolul „soft power" in diplomatia publica chineza. In: Studia securitatis, 2013, nr. 1. p. 71.

[97] B. Courmont, Les outils du softpower chinois. In : Observatoire geostrategique de l'information", 5 juillet 2011, p. 12, http://www.iris-france.org/docs/kfm_docs/docs/2011-07-12-diplomatie-publique-softpower.pdf (accessed 12. 03.12)

[98] J. Wu. Past, Present and Future. In: China Security, Vol. 4, nr. 3, Summer 2008, p. 14.

China's diplomacy is hopeful to attract foreign public, by promoting its positive aspects, which are based on the important fact that China is a model UN member that did not have recourse to aggression for solving international issues. China's government believes that the 'peaceful development' is the way for building a 'harmonious world'.

China guarantees that its status is the one of a 'developing country' and it is not a threat for the 'developed world'[99]. However, such strategy will be increasingly hard to apply, considering the fast growth of China's economy and influence. China's external discourse is in full development.

The Dean of Qinghua University, Yan Xuetong, characterizes China as an intermediate and well-balanced state that is different from the other three countries of the BRIC group (Brazil, Russia, India and China). The Chinese officials do not hesitate to use harsh terms against the foreign attempts to denigrate the pillars of China's sovereignty, the legitimacy of the Communist party or the Tibet, Xinjiang or Taiwan issues, which are rather sensitive topics as they touch on the primary China's principle – "united China». China often warned other countries "not to interfere with its internal affairs" because "China is following its own development road" that has "Chinese specificities"[100].

China uses various *events* and *festivals* to promote image. The Olympic Games from 2008 and the Shanghai Universal Exhibition from 2010, show the importance of the international events in the strategy of the Chinese public diplomacy.

The Ministry of Culture of the People's Republic of China and various private institutions organize many cultural events, for example: the Year of Chinese Culture in France, in 2003; the festival 'China Now', in 2008, in Great Britain; 'Europalia China art festival', in 2009, in many European countries; or China's participation, as a honored guest, at the Book Fair from Frankfurt, where China succeeded to attract an important public in Europe, due to the cultural event diplomacy.

In addition, *exchange programs* have been encouraged within China's public diplomacy[101]. Compared with the US exchange programs, Chinese exchange programs does not play a decisive role in the Chinese public diplomacy. A major impediment to the success of exchange programs is Chinese language.

---

[99] China's Peaceful Development Road. http://eng.chinalaw.com.tw/Wbk/display.asp?id=51&keyword (accessed 12.03.12)

[100]Panta R. Rolul „soft power" in diplomatia publica chineza. In: Studia securitatis, 2013, nr. 1. p. 75.

[101] I. D'Hooghe. The Rise of China's Public Diplomacy. In: Clingendael Diplomacy Papers, 2007, nr. 12, p. 30http://www.clingendael.nl/publications/2007/20070700_cdsp_paper_hooghe.pdf (accessed 28.04.12)

To promote Chinese language were created *Confucius institutions*. The creation and spreading of Confucius institutions represent a boost for the Chinese public diplomacy. One of the first cultural centers, 'Hanban' – the national office to learn the Chinese language as a foreign language, opened in Seoul in 2004. Today, there are more than 500 such centers in the world.

The Confucius Institutes are the main structures for China. In order to achieve the public diplomacy objectives, these centers promote the Chinese language and culture. They also aim to create strategic alliances with business institutions, governments and other structures which are interested to establish stronger and more productive links with China and the world Chinese Diaspora[102].

Confucius Institute is one of the best ways to promote China's image worldwide. In 2004, a pilot Institute was opened in Uzbekistan and Seoul, and in 2011 there were 300 institutions in 88 countries, inclusively the USA. By 2020 Beijing purposes to open more than 1000 pilot – institutions.

China founded a considerable number of Confucius Institutes in Europe, 10 in France, 9 in Germany, 27 in Great Britain. At present it is early to know if these cultural centers will really promote China. The Chinese Prime Minister Wen Jiabao mentioned that the academic exchanges realized by Confucius Institute represent 'a link between heart and spirit' and an important way to project country's image[103].

Inspiring form Hollywood, Beijing developed the film industry, but it does not have the same freedom of expression like in other states. The State Administration of Radio, Film, and Television of China[104] ensure that the Chinese productions do not affect China's image outside of the country. The goal is to glorify China and its history through the cinematography. In countries where China would diplomatic missions are organized Chinese Film Festival.

In addition to culture, there is a specific item for the Chinese public diplomacy - *hard and soft powers are inseparable and complimentary*[105]. Such conception is old and can be found in the work "Art of War" after Sun Tzu. Highly esteemed and appreciated by Chinese, Sun Tzu considered that military action was a component – but not the most important – of the concept of security. From the standpoint of the

---

[102]G. Rawnsley. China Talks Back – Public Diplomacy and Soft Power for the Chinese Century. In: Handbook of Public Diplomacy. New-York: Routledge, 2009 , p. 284.
[103] R. Panta. Rolul „soft power" in diplomatia publica chineza. In: Studia securitatis, 2013, nr. 1. p. 77.
[104]State Administration of Radio, Film & Television (SARFT). http://www.chinaproject.de/Medien/State_Administration_of_Radio_TV.htm (accessed 18.05.14)
[105] M. Bassan. Le soft-power chinois en Afrique. In: Fiche de l'Irsem", 2012, nr. 13, p. 3. http://www.irsem.defense.gouv.fr (accessed 18.05.13)

Chinese researchers, soft power fosters hard power while hard power represents and sustains soft power development[106].

Another specific item for the Chinese public diplomacy was influenced by China's economic development. In other words, the Chinese consider that power is also of economic nature just as it is of political and military nature. Chinese soft power's version seems to have a larger meaning than the concept of 'soft power' as the Chinese do not conceive the economy as a distinct sphere of the politics. The Chinese leaders and a large number of scientists consider that the economy is the continuation of the politics through different means[107]. According to the conception of P. André, the strength of an economic power does not lie in the threatening intervention, but, on the contrary, in the threatening non-intervention. The Chinese capitalism is a state-led capitalism aiming at profit-making, as well as at the constant economic development.

Applying the soft power is one of the strategic elements of China's external policy abroad, particularly in Africa[108]; it is justified by the economic and diplomatic needs, that is, by the will to act as an attractive political partner for the African countries. In addition, it should be noted that there is an intention of minimizing the concept of 'China threat' at the regional and global level.

J. Kurlantzick considers that Beijing's resolve to focus its politics on Africa is not accidental. In the same time, China holds a strongly leading conceptual position in Africa, mainly in terms of fighting poverty, and, secondly, China cannot match the harsh political competition with the United States as the Chinese military capacities are limited, while the United States military potential is dominating the African continent[109].

The manner of communication and information

The appointment of Zhao Qizheng as Ministry of State Administration of Film, Radio and Television of People's Republic of China entailed a radical change in the manner Beijing was approaching the official information.

---

[106] R. Panta. Rolul „soft power" in diplomatia publica chineza. In: Studia securitatis, 2013, nr. 1. p. 68.

[107] P. André. La notion d'état dans la pensée politique chinoise et ses conséquences sur la scène internationale. p. 448. http://www.youscribe.com/catalogue/rapports-et-theses/savoirs/sciences-humaines-et-sociales/la-notion-d-etat-dans-la-pensee-politique-chinoise-et-ses-1524848 (accessed 28.04.12)

[108] M. Bassan M. Le soft-power chinois en Afrique. In: Fiche de l'Irsem", 2012, nr. 13, p. 4. http://www.irsem.defense.gouv.fr (accessed 18.05.13)

[109] J. Kurlantzick. China's Soft Power in Africa. In: Soft Power. China's Emerging Strategy in International Politics". London: Lexington Books, 2009, p. 165-183.

Zhao introduced a more Western-like and opener style as he doubled the frequency of the press conferences and appealed to the Chinese officials for becoming opener in their communication with foreign journalists[110].

We noticed a new relationship with the media of Chinese ambassadors. When coming to a diplomatic mission the Chinese diplomats establish wider relationships with local media. This is a necessity of contemporary public diplomacy. Chinese diplomats are not reticent anymore to organize press conferences during visits abroad[111].

The public declarations play increasingly a bigger role in the awareness strategy of the target – groups. On Chinese embassy websites in the world are published interviews and public declarations of Chinese Ambassador.

At the same time foreign journalists invited more often to official events in China. The annual sessions of the National People's Congress and the Advisory Political Conference of the Chinese People from March 2007, marked a historic event authorizing the foreign journalists to speak with the political persons without consulting in advance the Official Press Center[112].

China invests a lot in the official media, in order to ameliorate its image in the world, which is the main element of the Chinese strategy. In January 2009 the Chinese Government spent 6, 8 billion dollars for the fortification of the international presence of Xinhua – its official press agency, and for opening a vast network of offices abroad. By 2020, its purpose is to arrive at 200. Xinhua operates 140 bureaus worldwide, 7 regional centers with 10 000 employees, which daily broadcast in 6 languages[113].

During the Cold War, China Radio International, the Chinese version of the Voice of America, founded in 1941, broadcasts in 56 foreign languages and 4 Chinese dialects. The creation of China Daily in 1981, and the English version of Global Times in 2009, marked an important stage in the expansion and professionalism of the official Chinese press in English.

[110] I. D'Hooghe. The Rise of China's Public Diplomacy. In: Clingendael Diplomacy Papers, 2007, nr. 12, p. 22 http://www.clingendael.nl/publications/2007/20070700_cdsp_paper_hooghe.pdf (accessed 28.04.12)
[111] L. Hou, M. Kaufmann. Séduire l'Europe: la diplomatie publique chinoise en action, partie 2. La fin et les moyens, 2011. http://www.china-institute.org/articles/Seduire_l_Europe_la_diplomatie_publique_chinoise_en_action2. (accessed 12.05.2012)
[112] L. Hou, M. Kaufmann. Séduire l'Europe: la diplomatie publique chinoise en action, partie 2. La fin et les moyens, 2011. http://www.china-institute.org/articles/Seduire_l_Europe_la_diplomatie_publique_chinoise_en_action2. (accessed 12.05.2012)
[113] R. Panta. Rolul „soft power" in diplomatia publica chineza. In: Studia securitatis, 2013, nr. 1. p. 70.

The international broadcasting of the Chinese television CCTV has experienced a significant expansion since 1992. The CCTV programs aim to promote the Chinese tourism and business environment[114]. It is very difficult to estimate the audience share of the International CCTV and its influence in the world.

The Chinese success in the media field can be observed in Africa, where CCTV News and Radio Beijing obtained an influence in many African states, replacing CNN as a first source of information.

China uses more and more the Internet to realize the public diplomacy objectives. The Information Office verifies the Chinese sites in English, which are created to inform the foreign public about China[115], especially those that refer to the Olympic Games and the Universal exhibition from Shanghai and Tibet. The most important institutions of the Chinese Government have official websites with detailed information about their activity, but for now, the Chinese successes in using the Internet remain behind their American competitors[116].

Like the US, China is encompassed by the concept of 'smart power', which means applying all the means available for a country (coercive diplomacy, economic sanctions, force, international institutions, and negotiations) for the purpose of implementing the "main strategy".

Beyond smart power, China's attitude can be regarded as a strategy of influence resorting to diplomacy, international institutions, international law and economic pressure in order not to oppose another superpower, but to hinder and increase the financial and political costs.

The Chinese intellectuals have come to the unanimous conclusion that the Western values (particularly, the American ones) have determined the way of functioning and shaped the main goals of the international organizations (WTO, IMF, WB, NATO). On one hand, the Chinese aspire to propose an alternative model to the model currently proposed by the U.S. On the other hand, they are willing to tailor the international regime to such model, which would bring advantages for China's national interests.

---

[114] G. D. Rawnsley. China Talks Back – Public Diplomacy and Soft Power for the Chinese Century. In: Handbook of Public Diplomacy. New-York: Routledge, 2009, p. 286.
[115] I. D'Hooghe/ The Rise of China's Public Diplomacy. In: Clingendael Diplomacy Papers, 2007, nr. 12, p. 32 http://www.clingendael.nl/publications/2007/20070700_cdsp_paper_hooghe.pdf (accessed 28.04.12)
[116]L. Hou, M. Kaufmann. Séduire l'Europe: la diplomatie publique chinoise en action, partie 2. La fin et les moyens, 2011. p. 6   http://www.china-institute.org/articles/Seduire_l_Europe_la_diplomatie_publique_chinoise_en_action2. (accessed 12.05.2012)

Beijing recognizes the interest and importance of the international institutions and organizations in global politics, but the integration in the international order offers opportunities to guarantee its interests[117]. To realize these objectives, China needs to increase the influence in WTO and IMF, because the importance of votes depends on the economic power. As other countries, China uses 'soft power' to propose its political agenda, in particular, in front of the United Nations Organization.

The status as a Security Council permanent membership permits China, not only to address the international policy files, but also to participate to their regulation[118]. China uses its privileged status within UNO to politically support its oil and gas suppliers. Iran and Sudan received support from China within the Security Council concerning the energetic questions or the defense of the non-intervention principle in the internal affairs of a State (China's interest concerning Taiwan and Tibet's problem). It can be seen a remarkable increase of China's participation to the peacekeeping operations, located on the African continent, for the benefit of the geostrategic interests. China participates to the UNO missions in Sudan, Occidental Sahara, Ethiopia, Eritrea, and Liberia.

Using SWOT analysis, we can say that China is trying to achieve the above-mentioned objectives; each of them has weaknesses and strengths. The weaknesses of China's public diplomacy lie in the protection of human rights, the issue of the minorities (Tibet) and the issue of China's reunification with Taiwan. Despite the visible activity of China's public diplomacy oriented at solving the said issues, no conclusive results have been achieved until now. In compensation, China has gained two strong points – its economic success and old culture – which helped China's public diplomacy, convey a positive image of the People's Republic of China.

In conclusion, we can mention that nowadays the speech concerning 'soft power' in China is developing. In China the debates on this topic are concentrated around the occidental one. Occidental model of soft power gave a remarkable function to the Chinese speech, especially in the tendency to promote the relativity idea of the ideology and culture, and to recognize the universality of the values and Chinese socio – political system.

---

[117] J. Ikenberry, The Rise of China China's Ascent, Power, Security and the Future of International Politics. New-York: Cornell University Press, 2008.
[118] T. de Swielande, La Chine et le « Soft power »: une manière douce de défendre l'intérêt national ?, mars 2009, p. 8. http://www.uclouvain.be/cps/ucl/doc/pols/documents/NA2-INBEV-UECH-FULL.pdf (accessed 12.05.2012)

Since 2007 'soft power' represents one of the elements of the Chinese external policy strategy abroad, especially in Africa. The Chinese power is based on economic and diplomatic goals. It purposes to decrease the existing conception concerning the 'Chinese threat' at the regional and global stage.

Chine aspires to the recreation of the international existing regime, proposing a development model different from that proposed by the USA. Its operation would bring advantages to the Chinese national interests and would contribute to the world peacekeeping.

The Chinese public diplomacy goals are: legitimate the communist power, attract the foreign investments and correct China's negative image. The diplomacy weaknesses are: the problem of human and minority rights (Tibet) and the reunification problem of China with Taiwan. The economic success and the ancient culture represent the strengths of the Chinese public diplomacy. China's culture is the priority of the public diplomacy not only for Europe but also for the entire world.

Unlike other states, the People's Republic of China uses more active the public diplomacy tools: public declarations, cultural diplomacy and international media.

4. The Russian public diplomacy between 'soft power' and 'hard power'

The collapse of the Soviet Union, the largest territory in the world, created a power space right in the center of Eurasia. In this context, Z. Brzezinski, affirmed that the disintegration of the soviet state in 1991 conditioned a big geopolitical confusion.

The new realities from the international political scene after 1989 – the dissolution of Warsaw Treaty and Soviet Union, the creation of Russian Federation as a successor of the former soviet superpower and the definition of its role in the new global configuration, inclusively in the post – soviet space, determined the leaders from Kremlin to adopt new strategies in the external policy in order to get the old status. The external policy has an essential characteristic: a reversed rapport between the ambitions of a 'superpower' and Moscow's actions field on an international stage.

The Russian Federation's main goal after the end of the 'Cold war'' was to regain the status of great power, which would ensure its participation to the world government. This strategy increased. If in 1990 the Russian Federation was ready to accept the occidental norms and values, after 2000 it tries to develop an alternative political and economic model, but credible in front of the liberal and democratic Occident[119].

If in the first decade, after the collapse of the Soviet Union, Moscow tried to maintain the 'disobedient' states under its influence, by the ethno – political conflicts remained as 'dowry' from the Soviet Union. From 2000, the Russian pressure on the CIS countries has diversified. To make the Community's states obey, the Russian Federation started to use the economic and energetic 'weapons' (hard power instruments).

The policy regarding the CIS countries members has reversed, from passivity or occasional activism to an aggressive and organized dynamic.

The separatism represented the first external policy experience in the relationships between the Russian Federation and the former Soviet Union republics. This operation was led by Kremlin even before the proclamation of independence of the

---

[119] Fr. Melloul. Développement de l'influence de la France sur la scène internationale, Une diplomatie publique à la française, 12 octobre 2010, p. 39.
http://directdumas.typepad.fr/files/influence_de_la_france_sur_la_sc_ne_internationale_f__melloul_oct_2010.pdf (accesed 12.03.12)

former Soviet Union republics and had to block the centrifugal processes from USSR and interdict the dissolution of the Soviet Union[120].

According to Security Strategy of the Russian Federation until 2020, approved by the presidential decree on 12th of May 2009, Russia's long – term goal is the global power status[121].

Soft power is a novelty for Russian foreign policy. Traditionally, before, the Soviet Union and now Russia prefers use hard power to achieve its interests in its sphere of influence. The Russian Federation gives preference to hard power elements: military items in Republic of Moldova (1992) and Georgia (1992 and 2008), economic sanctions (gas crisis in Ukraine, ban of Moldovan and Georgian wines), and propagandistic actions etc.

We can identify three factors that determined the use of Russian public diplomacy.

1.   *The Russian Federation doesn't have a positive image in Occident.*

It is characterized like having an authoritarian political regime, where corruption increases, and press freedom is limited: journalists are often assassinated, and the neighbors under energy pressure. Americans and Europeans have a particularly negative image of Moscow's record on civil liberties. Roughly three-quarters or more in Germany, France, the U.S., Poland, Spain, the UK and Italy think Russia does not respect personal freedoms[122].

A report of the German Federal Office of Constitution protection from June 2010 mentions the Russian Federation as a potential source of cyber-attack and industrial espionage for German companies[123].

According to an annual survey, mentioned by T. Kastoueva – Jean, realized by International Center for public opinion study Globe Scan, with its headquarters in Toronto, for BBC and the Program for studying the international politics attitude (PIPA), from the University of Maryland, 42% of respondents from 21 countries considered that Russian plays a negative role in the world and only 30% of them expressed the opposite. The Russian Federation ranks the 5th place from the end, before Iran (55% and 17%), Pakistan (53% and 17%), Israel (51% and 21%) and North of Korea (48% and 20%). The biggest reticence towards Russia was noticed in

---

[120] R. Panta. Politica externa a Rusiei post-sovietice intre hard power si soft power. In: Stiinte politice, relatii internationale, studii de securitate, 2013, p. 324.

[121] Russia's national Security Strategy to 2020. http://rustrans.wikidot.com/russia-s-national-security-strategy-to-2020 (accessed 1.08.2014).

[122]Russia's Global Image Negative amid Crisis in Ukraine. http://www.pewglobal.org/2014/07/09/russias-global-image-negative-amid-crisis-in-ukraine/ (accessed 1.08.2014)

[123] T. Kastoueva – Jean. Soft power russe: discurs, outils, impact. Paris: IFRI, 2010. p. 5.

the countries as: Germany – 70%, France – 66%, USA – 64%, Turkey – 64%, Great Britain – 55%, Spain – 55%, and Canada – 54% [124].

The idea that Russia's degrading image influences negatively its economic interest, spread among the Russian elites, because the international negative image was in contradiction with the economic interests of the Russian Government which aimed to promote the country's image, considered a classical power, able to turn, in the shortest time, into an economic power.

The country's image is an important capital, which contributes to consolidate the state's geopolitical status abroad[125], in order to provide security, protection and promotion of the national interests. For the public diplomacy it is essential not only the transmission of their point of view, but building a trustful relationship with the foreign audience[126].

1. The orange Revolution from Ukraine (2004).

The awareness of the soft power importance in the Russian foreign policy was boosted by the orange revolution from Ukraine. In the Bulgarian political scientist's opinion Ivan Krastev, this revolution represented for Russia like the 11th of September 2001 for the USA, an event which modified the Russian approach concerning the external policy[127].

The revolution from Ukraine was a real psychological shock. The Russian elites did not believe that the non-governmental organizations were able to organize a revolt in the Ukrainian society. After this event, in Russia began to be analyzed the role of NGOs in public diplomacy

2. Economy growth in 2004 – 2008, which promoted the investments in the field.

Since his first presidential mandate, Vladimir Putin has expressed the intention to continue to ensure for Russian Federation its role of central integration power in the post-soviet area, by tools as 'soft power' and 'public diplomacy'.

At the same time Russian Federation continued to use hard power: the gas crisis in Ukraine (January 2006 and 2009), the war in Georgia (august 2008) and crisis in Ukraine (2014-2015). This is an essential characteristic of Russian foreign policy, and is significant when we examine the Russian public diplomacy.

---

[124] Rossija upala v glazah drugih stran.
http://news.bbc.co.uk/hi/russian/international/newsid_7873000/7873561.stm (accessed 1.03.2013).
[125] K.S. Gadzhiev, Imidzh kak instrument kul'turnoj gegemonii în "Mirovaja jekonomika i mezhdunarodnye otnoshenija",nr.12/2007, p. 6
[126]3. Kononenko, V.A., Sozdat' obraz Rossii? în "Rossija v global'noj politike", nr.2/ 2006, vol. 4. p.195.
[127]T. Kastoueva – Jean. Soft power russe: discurs, outils, impact. Paris: IFRI, 2010. p. 5.

A long time in the lexicon of Russian external policy there were used two terms of diplomacy, <<*publichinaya* (public)>> and <<*obshestvenaya* (social)>>. Nevertheless, these two terms must be used with prudence. We live in an era of global communication and transformation. The word << *obshestvenaya* >> can be translated in other languages by 'socia', 'civil', or 'popular'. By 'social diplomacy', the Russian scientists refer to the NGO's diplomacy[128].

This is a reminiscence of the Soviet Union time, when the activities of the organizations involved in international exchange were operated inside of a single state, with a single ideology. The parallel use of the terms << *publichinaya* >> and << *obshestvenaya* >> is a period exceeded by the Russian historiography. The Decree 'concerning the measures of external policy implementation of the Russian Federation' signed by the president Vladimir Putin on May 7th 2012, ends the dispute. Since then the using term is 'public diplomacy'.

Trying to implement public diplomacy activities, the political leaders from the Russian Federation, and the scientists researched about the Soviet Union history, looking for using public diplomacy tools during the Cold war, but the Soviet Union did not have a public diplomacy where the Russian Federation could currently inspire from, we would rather speak about cultural diplomacy and propaganda.

In April 1925, a public organism was created in the Soviet Union – the Society for cultural relations with the foreign countries *(Vsesaiuznaya obshestva culturnoy sveazy s zagranitsey - VOCS)*, which gathered remarkable people from different fields: science, literature, arts, education and sport. The aim of this organization was to familiarize the foreign countries audience with the soviet culture realizations and promote the Soviet people's culture abroad, contributing to friendship development and strengthening, and reciprocal comprehension with peoples from the Soviet Union and other states[129].

In 1958 the VOCS was replaced with *Soyuz sovetskih obshestv drujbi*, but in 1992 was created the Russian Association of International Cooperation *(Rosiiskaya Asotsiatsia mejdunarodnavo sotrudnichestva)*.

Two years later, was founded the Russian Center for International scientific and cultural cooperation of the Russian Federation Government – *Rosiskii tsenter*

---

[128] T. Zonova. Publichnaja diplomatija i ee aktory. http://russiancouncil.ru/inner/?id_4=681#top (accessed 12.03.13)
[129]Vsesojuznoe obshhestvo kul'turnoj svjazi s zagranicej
http://dic.academic.ru/dic.nsf/bse/76356/%D0%92%D1%81%D0%B5%D1%81%D0%BE%D1%8E%D0%B7%D0%BD%D0%BE%D0%B5 (accessed 24.04.13)

mejdunarodnavo nauchinavo I culiturnovo sotrudnichestva (Roszarybejtsentr). The Russian Center for International scientific and cultural cooperation – *Roszarybejtsentr* received the status of public organism under the patronage of the Russian Federation Government, in order to culturally and scientifically cooperates with foreign countries[130].

In the Russian Federation the problem of the country's image was included for the first time in the *External Policy Conception,* adopted by the parliament and promulgated by the Russian president on 28th of June, 2000. In this document, the primary objective was to present to the public the exact information concerning the Russian Federation's positions towards the international major problems, its initiations and actions of external policy, and the realizations in the Russian science and culture field[131].

In the plenary session with the ambassadors and permanent representatives of the Russian Federation, from 12th of July, Vladimir Putin mentioned the image the Russian Federation has in the world is far from the reality, being the result of a discredit campaign.

That's why the main goal of the Russian diplomacy is to create a favorable image abroad.

Since 2004 in the Russian Federation have been elaborated different projects, in order to create an attractive image – instruments of Russian public diplomacy.

1.   Role of the media

In December 2005 appeared the *Russia Today,* which broadcasts in English during 24 hours. On 4th of May 2007, the *Rusia Ali Laum* broadcasts in Arab language for the states from Near East and North of Africa.

From 2007, the newspaper *Rosiiscaia gazeta* has been publishing supplements in partnership with international media, with more than 3 million copies.

The magazine *Russia in Global Affairs* has an English electronic version. The interviews with V. Putin and D. Medvedev are regularly translated and published in the Western media[132].

All the events that value the Russian Federation are in the media, for example: the 60th anniversary from the victory against the fascism (creation of a website dedicated

---

[130] Istorija. http://www.russiefrance.org/ru/nous/historique.html (12.03.13)

[131]Koncepcija vneshnej politiki Rossii ot 28 ijunja 2000 goda. http://www.mid.ru (accessed 26.02.13)

[132] R. Panta. Politica externa a Rusiei post-sovietice intre hard power si soft power. In: Stiinte politice, relatii internationale, studii de securitate, 2013, p. 324.

to the anniversary, the military parades which present the latest military equipments and the contribution to promote the image of the Russian Federation as a military power), the Russian victory at Eurovision in 2008, or the Sochi 2014 Olympic Games.

The Great War for Homeland Defense (the Russian name during the World War II where the Soviet Union fought against Germany), and the victory of the Soviet Union in the World War II, are the main elements of dignity and national identity of the Russian public diplomacy, being rejected any attempts of revision and reinterpretation of these events.

In May 2009, the Russian president V. Putin signed a Decree concerning the creation of a Commission which would prevent the falsification of the history in the detriment of the Russian Federation interests. The commission, composed from historians and senior officials, aims to prevent the revision of the geopolitical results of the World War II, which could serve as a basis for the political, financial and territorial claims.

One of the most important tools of the Russian Federation in the CIS countries is the Russian media, which represents an important source of information for the majority of the population from the former Soviet Union countries. If previously the media was focusing on newsletters, analytical programs, nowadays, it is all about concerts, sportive events, and very popular movies. The popularity and credibility in these tools represent the nostalgia for the Soviet period. It is certain that soft power elements were presented within the Russian foreign policy until 2008, but after this year it is given a more important role[133].

1. *Rossotrudnecestvo* - Federal Agency for the CIS countries' problems, of the compatriots living abroad

In March 2005, within the presidential administration, was created a special Direction, for international and cultural cooperation with the foreign states. The nomination of Modest Kolerov, a specialist in political technologies, confirms that this direction is a reaction to the Orange Revolution from Ukraine and its vocation is to promote the Russian influence in the post – soviet space. In October 2008, a new public structure replaced the *Roszarybejtsentr*. Was founded the Federal Agency for the CIS countries' problems, of the compatriots living abroad – *Rossotrudnecestvo*, in

---

[133]Panta R. Politica externa a Rusiei post-sovietice intre hard power si soft power. In: Stiinte politice, relatii internationale, studii de securitate, 2013, p. 328.

accordance, with the Decree nr. 1315 of the Russian president, from September 6th 2008, The Agency aims to develop the cooperation in the humanitarian field.

In a short time, the Agency succeeded to create a development strategy, a normative base, and established partnerships with Russian ministries, nongovernmental organizations and departments. The Agency's main objective is to stimulate the Russian Federation policy in the cultural – humanitarian field, both in the former Soviet Union space, and in the world.

The Agency, together with the Ministry of Education and Science of the Russian Federation, elaborated the Federal Target Program ,,Russian Language for 2011 – 2015''[134], approved by the Scientific Coordinating Council. The activities of the Agency are primarily focused on fortifying a modern Russia and expanding the cultural centers throughout the rest of the world. By 2020, there will be open more than 100 Russian Science and Culture Centers. They are the principles of the Russian public diplomacy, which reinforce friendship between nations.

2. Different organizations, financed by the state.

One of them is *Russkii Mir*, founded in 2007 by the Ministry of Foreign Affairs and the Ministry of Education and Research in order to promote the Russian culture and language. The organization is an equivalent of British Council or Confucius Institute, which helped to open Russian centers in 30 states. The responsibility of these organizations is to organize thematic weeks, dedicated to the Russian culture, language, cinema, sports, festivals, concerts[135]. These organizations have a regional vocation and cooperate with the member states of the Commonwealth of Independent States.

3. The Russian Orthodox Church

Certain Russian experts consider that 'soft power' of Russia is influenced by the Russian Orthodox Church. For many scientists, the Russian Orthodox Church remains a state institution, supported by the Russian Government[136].

On 27th of March 2007 in *'Obzor vneshnei politike Rossiiskoi Federatsii'[137]* for the first time within the Russian foreign policy, appeared the term of humanitarian

---

[134] Federal'naja celevaja programma «Russkij jazyk» na 2011-2015 gody. http://svn.rs.gov.ru/node/465 (accessed 12.12.14)
[135] Rol' russkogo jazyka v mire: novye vyzovy i reshenija. http://www.mid.ru (accessed 26.02.13)
[136] T. Kastoueva – Jean. Soft power russe: discurs, outils, impact. Paris: IFRI, 2010. p. 5.
[137]Obzor vneshnei politike Rossiiskoi Federatsii.
http://www.mid.ru/brp_4.nsf/0/3647DA97748A106BC32572AB002AC4DD (accessed 26.02.13)

direction which includes: human rights defense, compatriots defense who live abroad, consular problems and cooperation in the cultural and scientific field.

The humanitarian direction is also present in the 'Foreign policy concept of the Russian Federation' from 2008, being defined as a set of political and administrative resources, instruments and approaches of the Russian foreign policy. They aim to influence certain states, groups, or international society in order to legitimate or obtain the political support for the Russian foreign policy[138].

The humanitarian organization for the Russian Federation in accordance with *'Obzor vneshnei politike Rossiiskoi Federatsii'* purpose to defend and legitimate the citizens and Russian compatriots rights, to expand the area of Russian language and culture communication, to consolidate the organizations of compatriots and to prohibit the revision of the history in the post soviet union countries.

The Institute of Contemporary Development from Russia (INSOR), mentions in the study 'The economic interests and Russia tasks in the CIS courtiers' that the Russian Federation has to give up the role of an 'older brother' and, the same time, to increase the economic assistance offered to the CIS countries. Otherwise the Russia's place will be taken by the European Union, China and other countries. The study launched in early March 2010, found the significant reduction of Russia's economic influence in the CIS countries, in favor of European Union and China[139].

Within the humanitarian dimension, a significant attention is given to the compatriots' protection. In accordance with the 'Federal Law of the national policy concerning the compatriots', the term of compatriot comprises four groups: citizens from the Russian Federation who permanently live abroad, people who lived in the Soviet Union and now live in the former Soviet Union republics, those who obtained the citizenship of the resident country and those without it, immigrants from Russia who obtained the Russian citizenship and have citizenship in the resident country or without it, descendents of all categories mentioned above, except the titular nation.

According to the same document, after the dissolution of the Soviet Union, millions of people met outside the borders of their homeland – *Russia*. Then appeared the concept of historical Homeland as part of the Russian World *(Ruskii Mir)*, considered a unique element of the human civilization. The compatriots have the role

---

[138] Koncepcija vneshnej politiki Rossijskoj Federacii 2008. http://kremlin.ru/acts/785 (accessed 26.02.13)
[139] R. Panta. Politica externa a Rusiei post-sovietice intre hard power si soft power. In: Stiinte politice, relatii internationale, studii de securitate, 2013, p. 328.

of spiritual, economic, and cultural partners of the Russian Federation[140]. The granting of the Russian citizenship to the residents from other countries enforced the consular relations.

If we refer to the cooperation in the cultural and scientific field, another characteristic of the humanitarian dimension, it has, as a primary objective, the prevention of the history reinterpretation in the post-soviet space. To realize this objective, there were created centers of the Foundation Ruskii Mir, which donate Russian literature books or history books.

The number of Russians in the CIS countries recorded a rebound after the disintegration of the Soviet Union. This could be explained by affirming the new independent states, promoting the national language (closing the Russian schools, and certain TV channels), and the problem of the Russian language being politicized. Only the Republic of Belarus granted the Russian language as a state language, in Kazakhstan and Kirgizstan it is one of the official languages[141].

The surveys organized in the CIS countries, reveal that the states still use very active the Russian media[142]. In Armenia, Kazakhstan, Kirgizstan, Republic of Moldova, Tajikistan, and Ukraine, more than three – fours of the population watch the Russian television, in the Republic of Belarus 96%, but in Georgia and Azerbaijan, where the access to the Russian networks is not direct, those are watched by half of the population[143].

The higher education is another important element of 'soft power', because it contributes to the formation of the future foreign economic, political and military elites, towards the country which contributed to their formation. The number of students from CIS, who study in the Russian Federation, represents more than half of the foreign students, but this flow decreases. Even the students from Kazakhstan, traditionally oriented towards Russia, prefer nowadays the Great Britain.

Conscious for that, the Russian government launched several reforms in this field, in order to compete on the international market of services. These reforms brought a first increase of 4, 3% in 2008, towards 2% in 2000. For the moment, as mentions

---

[140] The humanitarian dimension of Russian Foreign policy toward Georgia, Moldova, Ukraine and the Baltic states, Riga, 2009. p, 21 www.geopolitika.lt/files/ (accessed 6.04.12)

[141] Tishkov A. Russkij jazyk i russkojazychnoe naselenie v stranah SNG i Baltii. B: Vestnik Rossijskoj akademii nauk, 2008, nr. 5, c. 417.

[142] Russkij jazyk v novyh nezavisimyh gosudarstvah. Moskva: Nasledie Evrazii, 2008. http://www.fundeh.org/publications/books/2/ (accessed 26.02.13)

[143] T. Kastoueva – Jean. Soft power russe: discurs, outils, impact. Paris: IFRI, 2010. p. 9.

Lebedeva, the higher education is not an instrument of 'soft power', because it does not have a clear and coherent program[144].

The education is exported through the commercial presence in the partner states, where are opened branches, or common universities. R. S. Muhametov considers that the branches network of the universities from Russia plays an important role in the realization of Russian compatriots' rights to study in Russian[145]. Nowadays, there are branches of Russian universities in almost all the CIS countries and Baltic States: the Lomonosov Moscow State University, the Gubkin Russian State University of Oil and Gas.

The universities branches from the Russian Federation have the following goal: develop the learning of Russian language and culture in other states, contribute to the preservation of Russian culture and language in the neighbor countries, support the operation of the Russian language in the CIS and Baltic countries, defend the compatriots' rights, inclusively that of studying in the native language, and reestablish the cultural – informational field in the post-soviet area. Currently, 165 500 people from 150 states are studying in 790 institutions from Russia, (80 thousand being from the CIS countries).

The budget the Russian Federation uses for the soft power tools is difficult to be precisely evaluated, because it is composed from various elements[146]. A few elements allow us to conclude that since 2004 the Russian Federation has invested in the soft power instruments, but these financial investments are inferiors than those from the USA, European States and China.

In September 2008, during a meeting with D. Medevedev, V. Nikonov, the president of *Ruskii Mir*, mentioned the organization's activities, and its weaknesses: lack of funds, a small number of Nongovernmental organizations involved in the activities, a dissuasive legislation and the bureaucratic obstacles which make difficult the activity of *Ruskii Mir*.

Within the Russian public diplomacy was necessary to develop the own sources of influence on the foreign public opinion, as well as to create a leading state body, in order to establish the strategy and tactic of the information ensurance of the foreign policy, and the coordination of the state bodies activity in the public diplomacy field.

---

[144] Lebedeva M. M. Vysshee obrazovanie kak potencial"mjagkoj sily" Rossii. B: Vestnik MGIMO", 2009. Nr. 6. p. 203.
[145] R. S. Muhametov. Kul'tura kak instrument vneshnej politiki Rossii. B: Izvestija Ural'skogo gosudarstvennogo universiteta, 2011, N 1(86), c. 194.
[146] T. Kastoueva – Jean. Soft power russe: discurs, outils, impact. Paris: IFRI, 2010. p. 21.

On February 3rd 2010, D. A. Medvedev signed the Decree concerning the creation of the public diplomacy Support Fund A. M. Gorceacov, which develop an intense campaign of popularization of the Russian diplomacy and promote an active implication of the nongovernmental organizations.

Role of the Internet in Russian public diplomacy

The Russian Federation is one of the most dynamic IT market in the world, and continues to increase. According to the data of the Public Opinion Fund, at the end of 2011, approximately 46% from the Russian population used the Internet[147], but in accordance with the study realized by the company TNS, the most accessed social network in 2011 was *VKontakte*, with 12 million visitors per day, followed by *Odnoklassniki (Одноклассники)*, with 7, 2 million people per day, and *Moi Mir (Мой мир)*, with 5, 3 million. The contribution of Internet to the national economy was approximately of 2% from GDP[148].

When Vladimir Putin came to Kremlin in 2000, the state control on the audiovisual and some printing press titles was noticed in the Russian Internet (named Runet). Between 2000 and 2008, Runet, including also the CIS countries and the Russian Diaspora, estimated to 27 million, has registered an annual average increase of 5 and receptively 14 times higher than in the Near East and Asia. Today, the Russian Federation is the biggest consumer of Internet in terms of percentage of web surfers in the world[149]. The Russian state is a web 'proactive actor' which aims to modify the national information space and broadcast favorable political messages.

The way of Internet control in the Russian Federation is similar to that used in China, and it aims to recreate the state's image on Internet. The Internet solves a double deficit of political governance and legitimacy. Firstly, the Russian territory stretching is an impediment in maintaining the national identity, the television plays a 'unifying' role, but its impact decreases, especially among young people. Secondly, Kremlin tries to use the interaction of governors – governed on Internet for introducing the horizontality in the verticality of the power by posting information about policy people[150].

---

[147] Internet v Rossii. Metodika i osnovnye rezul'taty issledovanija. Analiticheskij bjulleten', 2011, Vesna, № 33. http://bd.fom.ru/pdf/Internet (31.08.12).
[148] Rossija onlajn: vlijanie interneta na rossijskuju jekonomiku. Otchet Boston Consulting Group. 2011. http://img.rg.ru/pril/article/48/57/59/000111333.pdf (accessed 31.08.12).
[149] J. Nocetti "e- Kremlin": pouvoir et Interne en Russie Paris: Ifri, 2011. p. 4.
[150] J. Nocetti "e- Kremlin": pouvoir et Interne en Russie Paris: Ifri, 2011. p. 5.

The Internet nationalization in Russian is original, because it supposes a series of governmental initiatives to determine the Russian Internet users to remain in the Russian cyberspace. In March 2010, it was proposed to create a research motor in order to 'answer to the state needs', 'facilitate the access to the secured information', and 'filtrate the web sites which display prohibited contents'[151].

Yandex is Russia's most popular search engine and most visited website but the does not have any interest to depreciate Yandex; the nationalization target would be Google. The capacity of Kremlin to build a credible concurrent for Google remains limited, because the American companies dispose of quasi – unlimited financial, technological, and juridical resources.

Unlike China and the US, there is no state body for coordinating the public diplomacy in Russia. The activities from this field are developed by the Ministry of Foreign Affairs, Ministry of Regional Development, Obcestvennaia Plata, Roszarubejtsent, RIA – Novosti, Russia Today, but there is no communication mechanism between them. The coordination of public diplomacy is administered by the top leaders, and the concrete indications are given to the representatives of media services.

According to the expert A. Dolinschi's opinion, the existed structure has also negative aspects: firstly, because of a large number of tasks, these persons find it difficult to systematically deal with public diplomacy, and secondly, this organization has a vertical character, that represents an impediment for the horizontal cooperation[152].

The existing connections are most of the time unidirectional, without being provided the elements interdependence. This scheme is efficient when it is periodically necessary the mobilization of all the possibilities of public diplomacy, in the context of some important events: G8 Summit, elections, army conflicts, but it is not efficient for a systematic coordination, altghout some elements have already cooperated between them (for example the Ministry of Foreign Affairs and Roszarubejtsent). This structure cannot ensure an efficient collaboration between the

---

[151]Rogovskij E. SShA: informacionnoe obshhestvo. Jekonomika i politika. Moskva: Mezhdunarod¬nye otnoshenija, 2008. 408 c.
[152] A. Dolinskij. Prakticheskie voprosy optimizacii rossijskoj publichnoj diplomatii. p. 6 http://www.russkiymir.ru/analytics/tables/news/119896/ (accessed 12.03.13)

elements, in lack of a coordination mechanism which would suppose the reverse link with the country's leadership, or the elements interdependence[153].

Besides the deficient characteristics, the nongovernmental organizations have a negative influence on the Russian Federation' s image abroad, and play an important role in its public diplomacy. A. Dolinschi considers that according to the American model, it is required an Agency for the public diplomacy which would coordinate the activities of the Russian public diplomacy.

Making a retrospective of the two decades of Russian foreign policy and forecasting the future, the policy document ,,Theses on Russian Foreign Policy 2012 – 2018'', published at the end of 2012 includes some necessary conclusions of this analysis.

From the moment when the international role of the Russian Federation was and is determined by the internal situation for the years 2012 – 2018, the main objectives of Russia's foreign policy have to be determined by its internal development. The main challenge that Russian Federation faces with in the first half of the 21st century is the deep and multidimensional modernization. The socio – economic and political modernization of the Russian Federation has, on the one hand, to increase the capacity of the Russian foreign policy, by creating additional opportunities, and on the other, to determine its priorities. It is very important to maintain a balance between the economic, social and humanitarian development, also the security dimension. These three fields should complete each other and not compete[154].

The authors of 'Theses of Foreign Policy' suggest promoting more active the modern means of communication. Another important resource would be the export of the educational services, which should include the creation of a more qualitative product and stimulation of the flow of students. Such a strategy should be elaborated by the participation of the Ministry of Foreign Affairs and the Ministry of Education, and by the identification of some niches. It is important that the Russian universities remain attractive for the neighbor states which the Russian Federation has integrationist economic relations and creates security systems with.

The science and technology would be another resource of the Russian soft power. In recent years, there were initiated a few federal projects. They aim to stimulate the innovation, the scientific, educational, and infrastructure projects, but the increase of

---

[153] A. Dolinskij. Prakticheskie voprosy optimizacii rossijskoj publichnoj diplomatii. p. 6 http://www.russkiymir.ru/analytics/tables/news/119896/ (accessed 12.03.13)
[154]Tezisy o vneshnej politike Rossii (2012 – 2018) p. 5. http://russiancouncil.ru/common/upload/RIAC_foreign_policy(1).pdf(accessed 12.03.13)

financial allocations did not lead to qualitative changes in the modernization of Russia's science and its integration in the global mechanism of scientific cooperation.

The Russian culture is an important element of soft power, but it should be promoted in an commercial way, by a common strategy of the Ministry of Foreign Affairs and Ministry of Culture, the targeted audiences are not only the CIS countries but also the main partners of the Russian Federation in the world – Europe, North America, China, India, Japan, Turkey. The Russian culture value has also to increase by interacting with the Russian Diaspora. The culture is closely related to the language, being necessary to continue to develop the education in the Russian language in the CIS countries, by revitalizing the slave universities, radio broadcast, TV and Internet in Russian.

An essential resource of the Russian Federation's soft power is considered the tourism, which Russia invests money for its development, but this development needs the elaboration of a national program of infrastructure.

The chronic problem for the Russian Federation was the incapacity to use the potential of the Russian Diaspora, especially in the Western countries. The obstacles that determined this thing before (the ideological nature of migration from Russia, the limited resources the state could allocate in this field, the lack of efficient communication channels), seem to have disappeared.

The Russian Federation foreign policy is based on some tools: the military force (including its nuclear composition), the energetic resources the great economies of the world need, the presence in the international organizations (the status of permanent member of the Security Council). The kit of tools should be extended to the new communication technologies, the research globalization, and the explosion of public diplomacy[155].

At the beginning of the third millennium, the Russian Federation showed its intention to continue to ensure the role of integrationist power in the post-soviet area, through soft power instruments and public diplomacy. In the first stage of their implementation (2004 – 2010), it was realized a lack of financial means, a low number of involved NGOs, a dissuasive legislation and bureaucratic obstacles, especially the lack of own sources of influence on foreign public opinion.

---

[155]Tezisy o vneshnej politike Rossii (2012 – 2018) p. 6.
http://russiancouncil.ru/common/upload/RIAC_foreign_policy(1).pdf(accessed 12.03.13)

Although, it was felt the need of creation of a state governing body, which would establish the strategies and tactics of foreign policy information ensurence, as well as the coordination of the state bodies activity in the public diplomacy field.

In conclusion, we can mention that the central axis of the Russian public diplomacy is to promote its image. For the first time the country's image problem was included in the foreign policy Conception in 2000. According to this document, it was expected the confirmation of the Russian Federation's role as a central integrationist power in the post-soviet area, through soft power tools and public diplomacy.

From 2004, in the Russian Federation, have been elaborated different projects for the creation of an attractive image. They started to promote the events which emphasize the country's image: the 60th anniversary Victory Day, the Russian victory at Eurovision in 2008, or the Sochi 2014 Olympic Games.

The Russian soft power instruments can be divided into 2 categories: those oriented towards the CIS countries (the Russian language, the Russian media space, the Russian Diaspora, the higher education), and those for the European states and the USA.

There is no state body to coordinate the public diplomacy in the Russian Federation: the activities from this field are conducted by the Ministry of Foreign Affairs, Ministry of Regional Development, Obshestvenaya Plata, Rosszarubejtsent, RIA – Novosti, Russia Today, but there is no coordination mechanism between them.

The creation of the A. M. Gorchakov Public Diplomacy Support Fund in 2010 represents an important step in the Russian public diplomacy's evolution. This institution conducts a campaign of Russian diplomacy's popularization and promotes a more active implication of nongovernmental organizations.

The Russian Federation repeats all the USA errors, committed in the revival process of its public diplomacy after the tragedy of September 11: the increasing number of channels of unidirectional communication and the approximate absence of the dialogue with the foreign auditors. In the consequence, the Russian foreign policy needs a full rethinking of public diplomacy as a cooperation instrument based on a bilateral dialogue and with a more active implication of the non – state actors.

The application of soft power strategies and concerns for the country's image abroad, did not stop the parallel manifestation of the Russian foreign policy, determined by 'hard power'.

5. Conclusions

This analysis helps us to conclude that every public diplomacy activity can be divided in three stages: reactive, proactive and creative.

The reactive stage, the main one, is based on communication through traditional diplomacy. Within it is developed the process of the state recognition abroad. No state can successfully organize public diplomacy activities without its international recognition by the other states and organization of a basic traditional diplomacy.

The proactive stage is centered on the idea of promoting the country's positive image through strategic communication. The communication process is composed from simple messages broadcast by media and within different cultural activities. It establishes strategies of public diplomacy. The elaboration of an efficient strategy includes the following elements: a list of a priority states, one or two clear messages, a target group to address to, and a communication strategy with others (beyond the governmental structure).

After analyzing the models of public diplomacy presented in this article, we could mention that one strategy of public diplomacy is not able to capture the attention of all the states. It is rational to select a group of states (geographically, neighbor states, or states – members of different organizations) and adopt the strategy of public diplomacy to their culture and interest.

The second stage which provides theoretical support to public diplomacy activities is preceded by the last stage, the longest and the most difficult. Its activities are oriented to a better understanding of the country and its national interests. There are many instruments. Some of them were taken by the states and adopted to the new context: cultural diplomacy, public declarations, media, and international broadcasting, etc.

The cultural diplomacy – is a component of the public diplomacy, successfully applied by all the analyzed states. If the activities of cultural diplomacy are well organized, it could be noticed the transition to the final stage within the activities of public diplomacy. There is created a link for the realization of public diplomacy's objectives. To facilitate this process, the public diplomacy has to be integrated into the public policy of the governmental agencies. It is necessary to take into account the audience attitudes and habits understanding, the priorities establishment (what is the purpose of this public policy? what kind of impact? at what level? how long?), and the choice of the message and broadcasting tools of the public policy.

Both the Chinese and American diplomacy dispose of such tradition. The American public diplomacy has its origin in the Declaration of Independence, in the identity of the USA, based on liberty, equality, democracy and human rights. These values are dedicated to the exportation and shared by other peoples from the world. If during the 'cold war' the purpose of the American public diplomacy was to understand, inform and influence the foreign audience in promoting the national interest, after the 11th of September 2001, it focused on favoring the common values and interests between the Americans and peoples from different countries.

The Chinese public diplomacy has been using its power of attraction for a few centuries. To promote the country's image abroad, China appeals to consensual values, susceptible to be shared as 'harmony' and 'peace'.

The Russian public diplomacy lacks this characteristic. The message the Russian Federation delivers abroad is a contradictory one. The Russian Federation wishes to develop 'soft power', but the first decision after the recognition of Abkhazia and South Ossetia was to establish military bases. Although it presents itself as an integrant part of the global political processes, the Russian Federation puts the accent on its own way of development and values that are not shared by other states.

The negative image accompanied by a scrambled message, makes the public diplomacy to be perceived abroad as a message intended to mask the ineffective reforms, and the recourse to 'hard power' in Ukraine in 2014, questions the credibility of the Russian soft power.

The American and Chinese models prove the necessity to institutionalize the public diplomacy. It does not mean to create a new agency, but to modify the existed structures and to orient them towards an interdepartmental working method.

By this we conclude – the success of the public diplomacy activities is determined by: the context where are developed the public diplomacy strategies, which must be adapted to the target audience; the disposed financial resources and the instruments used to realize this activity. The public diplomacy tools and means must be permanently actualized and adjusted to the new information technologies.

Bibliography:

1. About the Office of Public Affairs. http://www.dhs.gov/about-office-public-affairs (accessed 04.02.15)

2. André P. La notion d'état dans la pensée politique chinoise et ses conséquences sur la scène internationale.http://www.youscribe.com/catalogue/rapports-et-theses/savoirs/sciences-humaines-et-sociales/la-notion-d-etat-dans-la-pensee-politique-chinoise-et-ses-1524848 (accessed 28.04.12)

3. Arpagian N. Washington aporte son soutien technique aux cyberdissidents. In: Observatoire géostratégique de l'information. Diplomatie publique, soft power...influence d'état", 2011, 5 juillet. http://www.iris-france.org/docs/kfm_docs/docs/2011-07-12-diplomatie-publique-softpower.pdf. (accessed 28.04.12)

4. Bardos. A. A. Public diplomacy: An old art, a new profession. In: Virginia Quarterly Review, 2001, 77 (3) p. 424-437.

5. Bassan M. Le soft-power chinois en Afrique. In: Fiche de l'Irsem", 2012, nr. 13, http://www.irsem.defense.gouv.fr (accessed 18.05.13).

6. Bellamy C., Weinberg A. Educational and cultural Exchanges to restore America's image. In: The Washington Quarterly, 2008, p. 55-68.

7. Blum U. Ubijstvo demokratii: operacii CRU i Pentagona v period holodnoj vojny. Moskva: Kuchkovo pole, 2013. 706 p.

8. Chernenko E. Internet - protokol'naja sluzhba Gosdepa. B: Kommersant, 2011, 15 sentjabrja, http://www.kommersant.ru/doc-rss/1773567 (accessed 31.08.2012).

9. China's Peaceful Development Road.
http://eng.chinalaw.com.tw/Wbk/display.asp?id=51&keyword (accessed 12.03.12)

10. Courmont B. Les outils du softpower chinois. In: Observatoire geostrategique de l'information, 5 juillet 2011, http://www.iris-france.org/docs/kfm_docs/docs/2011-07-12-diplomatie-publique-softpower.pdf (accessed 12. 03.12).

11. Courmont B. Chine, la grande séduction: essai sur le soft power chinois. Paris: Choiseul, 2009. http://www.diploweb.com/Chine-La-grande-seduction-Essai.html (accessed 28.04.12)

12. Cull N. China's Propaganda and Influence Operations, its Intelligence Activities that Target the United States and its Resulting Impacts on US National Security. Testimony before the US-China. In: Economic and Security Review Commission Hearing", 30 April 2009.

http://www.uscc.gov/hearings/2009hearings/transcripts/09_04_30_trans/09_04_30_tr ans.pdf (accessed 24. 06. 2012)

13. Cull. N. The Cold War and the United States Information Agency: American Propaganda and Public Diplomacy, 1945-1989. Cambridge: Cambridge University Press, 2008. 580 p.

14. Cvetkova N.A. Programmy web 2.0. v publichnoj diplomatii SShA. B: SShA i Kanada: Jekonomika, politika, kul'tura, 2011, no. 3, p. 109-122.

15. Conte C. La diplomatie culturelle française: La culture face à de nouveaux enjeux ? Toulouse: IEP, 2008.   http://www.interarts.net/descargas/interarts678.pdf. (accessed 18.05.13)

16. D'Hooghe I.The Rise of China's Public Diplomacy. In: Clingendael Diplomacy Papers, 2007, nr. 12,
http://www.clingendael.nl/publications/2007/20070700_cdsp_paper_hooghe.pdf (accessed 28.04.12)

17. de Swielande T. La Chine et le « Soft power »: une manière douce de défendre l'intérêt national ?, mars 2009
http://www.uclouvain.be/cps/ucl/doc/pols/documents/NA2-INBEV-UECH-FULL.pdf(accessed 12.05.2012)

18. Demidov O. Social'nye setevye servisy v kontekste mezhdunarodnoj i nacional'noj bezopasnosti. B: Indeks bezopasnosti, 2013, Vesna, nr. 1 (104), c. 65 - 76.

19. Devirieux M. Étude et critique du concept de diplomatie publique. In : Jurnal of Policy Studies, winter, 2011. p. 58-71.

20. Djerejian Ed. Changing Minds, Winning Peace: A New Strategic Direction for U.S. Public Diplomacy in the Arab & Muslin World.
http://www.state.gov/documents/ organization/24882.pdf (accessed 14.08.12).

21. Dolinskij A. Diskurs o publichnoj diplomatii. In: Mezhdunarodnye processy", 2011, nr. 3. http://www.intertrends.ru/twenty-fifth/008.htm (accessed 04.02.15)

22. Dolinskij A. Prakticheskie voprosy optimizacii rossijskoj publichnoj diplomatii.http://www.russkiymir.ru/analytics/tables/news/119896/   (accessed 12.03.13)

23. Federal'naja celevaja programma «Russkij jazyk» na 2011-2015 gody. http://svn.rs.gov.ru/node/465 (accessed 12.12.14)

24. Filimonov G. "Mjagkaja sila" kul'turnoj diplomatii SShA. Moskva: RUDN, 2010. 216 p.

25. Gadzhiev K.S. Imidzh kak instrument kul'turnoj gegemonii în "Mirovaja jekonomika i mezhdunarodnye otnoshenija", nr.12/2007, p. 3-14.

26. Galal. I. The History and Future of US Public Diplomacy. In: Global Media Journal, 2005, vol. 4. http://lass.purduecal.edu/cca/gmj/fa05/graduatefa05/gmj-fa05gradinv-galal.htm (accessed 12.01.14).

27. Gilboa E. Public Diplomacy in the Information Age. http://icp-forum.gr/wp/wp-content/uploads/2008/12/gilboa-lecture-athens-jan-2009.pdf. (accessed 18.12.13)

28. Gregory B. American Public Diplomacy: Enduring Characteristics, Elusive Transformation: In: Hague Journal of Diplomacy, 2011, nr. 6, p. 351-372.

29. Gregory B. Public Diplomacy and National Security: Lessons from the U.S. Experience. In: Small Wars Journal, 2008, august. www.smallwarsjournal.com (accessed 11.06.2013).

30. GregoryB. Not Your Grandparent's Public Diplomacy (Ottawa : Public Diplomacy Retreat Department of Foreign Affairs, November 30, 2005). p. 5-7
    https://www.gwu.edu/~smpa/faculty/documents/PDRetreat_000.pdf

31. Guceac I. Porcescu. S. Diplomatia publica – componenta indispensabila a discursului extern in conditiile globalizarii. In: Akademos, martie 2010, nr. 1(16), p. 7.

32. Hentea. C. Armele care nu ucid. Bucuresti: Nemira, 2004. p. 88.

33. Holbrooke R. "Get the message out," Washington Post, October 28, 2001. http://www.washingtonpost.com/wp-dyn/content/article/2010/12/13/AR2010121305410.html (accessed 5.10.2014).

34. Hughes K. "Waging Peace": A New Paradigm for Public Diplomacy. In: Mediterranean Quarterly", 2007, p. 18-37.

35. Hoffman D. Beyond Public Diplomacy. In: Foreign Affairs, 2002, march/april. www.foreignaffairs.com/articles/57813/david-hoffman/beyond-public-diplomacy (accessed 5.10.13).

36. Hou L., Kaufmann M. Séduire l'Europe: la diplomatie publique chinoise en action. partie 3. La stratégie chinoise porte-t-elle ses fruits?, http://www.china-institute.org/articles/Seduire_l_Europe_la_diplomatie_publique_chinoise_en_action3 . (accessed 28.04.12)

37. Hou L., Kaufmann M. Séduire l'Europe: la diplomatie publique chinoise en action, partie 2. La fin et les moyens, 2011. http://www.china-

institute.org/articles/Seduire_l_Europe_la_diplomatie_publique_chinoise_en_action2
. (accessed 12.05.2012)

38. Ikenberry J. The Rise of China China's Ascent, Power, Security and the Future of International Politics. New-York: Cornell University Press, 2008.

39. Internet v Rossii. Metodika i osnovnye rezul'taty issledovanija. Analiticheskij bjulleten', 2011, Vesna, № 33. http://bd.fom.ru/pdf/Internet (31.08.12).

40. Istorija. http://www.russiefrance.org/ru/nous/historique.html (12.03.13)

41. Kastoueva – Jean T.. Soft power russe: discurs, outils, impact. Paris: IFRI, 2010. 31 p.

42. Koncepcija vneshnej politiki Rossii ot 28 ijunja 2000 goda. http://www.mid.ru (accessed 26.02.13)

43. Koncepcija vneshnej politiki Rossijskoj Federacii 2008. http://kremlin.ru/acts/785 (accessed 26.02.13)

44. Kononenko V.A. Sozdat' obraz Rossii? în "Rossija v global'noj politike", nr.2/ 2006, vol. 4. p.192-201.

45. Kurlantzick J. China's Soft Power in Africa. In: Soft Power. China's Emerging Strategy in International Politics". London: Lexington Books, 2009, p. 165-183.

46. Layne. Ch. Pacea iluzorie: marea strategie americana din 1940 pana in prezent. Iasi: Polirom, 2011. 360 p.

47. Le Corre Ph. La Chine, nouvel acteur des relations internationales. In: Etudes, 2006, nr. 10, p. 307-318.

48. Lebedeva M. M. Vysshee obrazovanie kak potencial"mjagkoj sily" Rossii. B: Vestnik MGIMO", 2009. Nr. 6. p. 200-205.

49. Lepri. Ch. Du "soft power" avant l'heure: 1 exemple de la Guerre froid, In: Observatoire geostrategique de l'information, 5 juillet, 2011. http://www.iris-france.org/docs/kfm_docs/docs/2011-07-12-diplomatie-publique-softpower.pdf (accessed 21.01.2012).

50. Leonard M. Stead C., Smewing C. Public Diplomacy. London: The Foreign Policy Centre, 2002. http://fpc.org.uk/fsblob/35.pdf. (accessed 8.10.13)

51. Lukov V.V. Internet kak instrument politicheskih tehnologij v SShA. B: SShA i Kanada: Jekonomika, politika, kul'tura, 2005, no. 5, c. 91-108.

52. Mazilu. D. Dreptul diplomatic si consular. București: Lumina Lex, 2009. 516 p.

53. Megali R. Puissance Chine. La stratégie d'affirmation internationale chinoise. www.defense.gouv.fr/irsem/publications/fiches/fiches-de-l-irsem.   (accessed 12.03.13)

54. Melloul Fr.   Développement de l'influence de la France sur la scène internationale, Une diplomatie publique à la française, 12 octobre 2010. http://directdumas.typepad.fr/files/influence_de_la_france_sur_la_sc_ne_internationa le_f__melloul_oct_2010.pdf (accesed 12.03.12)

55. Miculescu. S. Relatii publice internationale in contextual globalizarii. Bucuresti: SNSPA, 2001. 150 p.

56. Muhametov R. S. Kul'tura kak instrument vneshnej politiki Rossii. B: Izvestija Ural'skogo gosudarstvennogo universiteta, 2011, N 1(86), c. 193-198.

57. Nakamura K. H., Weed M. C. U.S. Public Diplomacy: Background and Current Issues, Congressional Research Service. www.crs.gov. (accessed 18.12.13)

58. National Security Strategy, may 2010. http://www.whitehouse.gov/sites/default/files/rss_viewer/national_security_strategy. pdf (accessed 21.03.14)

59. Nye J. Soft Power: The means to success in world politics. New York: Public Affairs, 2004. 208 p.

60. Nocetti J. "e- Kremlin": pouvoir et Interne en Russie Paris: Ifri, 2011. 26 p.

61. Nocetti J. La diplomatie d'Obama à l'épreuve du Web 2.0. In: Politique étrangère, 2011, nr. 1, p. 157-179.

62. Obzor vneshnei politike Rossiiskoi Federatsii. http://www.mid.ru/brp_4.nsf/0/3647DA97748A106BC32572AB002AC4DD (accessed 26.02.13)

63. Panova. E.P. Vysshee obrazovanie kak potencial mjagkoj vlasti gosudarstva. B: Vestnik MGIMO-Universiteta, 2011, № 2 (15). c. 157-181.

64. Panta R . Rolul diplomatiei publice in securitatea nationala a SUA. In: Studia securitatis, 2012, nr. 3. p. 34-46.

65. Panta R. Politica externa a Rusiei post-sovietice intre hard power si soft power. In: Stiinte politice, relatii internationale, studii de securitate, 2013, p. 321-332.

66. Panta R. Rolul „soft power" in diplomatia publica chineza. In: Studia securitatis, 2013, nr. 1. p. 64 -78.

67. Panta R. Rolul diplomatiei publice in securitatea nationala a SUA. In: Studia securitatis, 2012, nr. 3. p. 34-46.

68. Panta. R. Public diplomacy- foreign policy instrument. In: Agora, Vol VI, 2012, nr. 1, p. 53-65.

69. Rata Al- Cl. Aplicatii ale internetului şi noua diplomatie digitala. In: Cultura şi comunicare, 2011, nr. 5.
   http://culturasicomunicare.com/pdf/2011/Rata%20Alex.pdf (accessed
   25.12.2013)

70. Rawnsley G. D. China Talks Back – Public Diplomacy and Soft Power for the Chinese Century. In: Handbook of Public Diplomacy. New-York: Routledge, 2009, p. 282-193.

71. Record number of foreign students to enrol in 2014.
http://www.universityworldnews.com/article.php?story=2014012916402922
(accessed 16.04.14)

72. Rogovskij E. SShA: informacionnoe obshhestvo. Jekonomika i politika. Moskva: Mezhdunarod¬nye otnoshenija, 2008. 408 c.

73. Rol' russkogo jazyka v mire: novye vyzovy i reshenija. http://www.mid.ru
   (accessed 26.02.13)

74. Rossija onlajn: vlijanie interneta na rossijskuju jekonomiku. Otchet Boston Consulting Group. 2011. http://img.rg.ru/pril/article/48/57/59/000111333.pdf
   (accessed 31.08.12).

75. Rossija upala v glazah drugih stran.
http://news.bbc.co.uk/hi/russian/international/newsid_7873000/7873561.stm
(accessed 1.03.2013).

76. Russia's Global Image Negative amid Crisis in Ukraine.
http://www.pewglobal.org/2014/07/09/russias-global-image-negative-amid-crisis-in-ukraine/ (accessed 1.08.2014)

77. Russia's national Security Strategy to 2020. http://rustrans.wikidot.com/russia-s-national-security-strategy-to-2020 (accessed 1.08.2014).

78. Russkij jazyk v novyh nezavisimyh gosudarstvah. Moskva: Nasledie Evrazii, 2008. http://www.fundeh.org/publications/books/2/ (accessed 26.02.13)

79. Ross Ch. Pillars of Public Diplomacy. In: Harvard International Review, 2006.
http://hir.harvard.edu/china/pillars-of-public-diplomacy (accessed 12.12.12)

80. Samujlov S.M. "Diplomatija preobrazovanij" Kondolizy Rajs i reformirovanie Gosdepartamenta SShA. B: Jekonomika, politika, kul'tura, 2008, Janvar'. No. 1. c. 17-33.

81. Scobell A. China's soft sell: Is the world buying? In: China Brief Volume. http://www.jamestown.org. (accessed 28.04.12)

82. Serban I. D. Diplomatia publica - instrument politic pentru SUA ca smart power - analiza cauzala. in: Research and science today, 2011, nr. 1, p. 79-91.

83. Shaum R. Noua diplomatie. Relatii internationale moderne. Bucuresti: Antet, 2004. 136 p.

84. State Administration of Radio, Film & Television (SARFT). http://www.chinaproject.de/Medien/State_Administration_of_Radio_TV.htm (accessed 18.05.14)

85. Szondi G. Public Diplomacy and Nation Branding, Conceptual Similarities and Differences (Discussion Papers in Diplomacy), Netherlands Institute of International Relations „Clingendael". peacepalacelibrary.nl (accessed 16.04.14)

86. Tănăsie P. Uzanțe diplomatice şi de protocol. Pitești: Independența economică, 2000. 335 p.

87. Tezisy o vneshnej politike Rossii (2012 – 2018). http://russiancouncil.ru/common/upload/RIAC_foreign_policy(1).pdf(accessed 12.03.13)

88. The humanitarian dimension of Russian Foreign policy toward Georgia, Moldova, Ukraine and the Baltic states, Riga, 2009. www.geopolitika.lt/files/ (accessed 6.04.12)

89. Tishkov A. Russkij jazyk i russkojazychnoe naselenie v stranah SNG i Baltii. B: Vestnik Rossijskoj akademii nauk, 2008, nr. 5, c. 415-423.

90. U.S. National Strategy for Public Diplomacy and Strategic Communication. Strategic Communication and Public Diplomacy Policy Coordinating Committee (PCC). June 2007. http://www.au.af.mil/au/awc/awcgate/state/natstrat_strat_comm.pdf. (accessed 04.02.14)

91. Vsesojuznoe obshhestvo kul'turnoj svjazi s zagranicej http://dic.academic.ru/dic.nsf/bse/76356/%D0%92%D1%81%D0%B5%D1%81%D0 %BE%D1%8E%D0%B7%D0%BD%D0%BE%D0%B5 (accessed 24.04.13)

92. Wang. J. Telling the American story to the world: The purpose of American public diplomacy in historical perspective. In: Public Relation revue", 2007, nr. 1(33). p. 21-30.

93. Wu J. Past, Present and Future . In: China Security, Vol. 4, nr. 3, Summer 2008.

94. Zaharna R. S. The network paradigm of Strategic Public Diplomacy. In: Policy Brief, 2005, vol 10, nr.1 april 2005.
https://www.american.edu/soc/faculty/upload/Network-Paradigm.pdf (accessed 12.04.13)

95. Zinov'eva E. Cifrovaja diplomatija, mezhdunarodnaja bezopasnost' i vozmozhnosti dlja Rossii. B: SShA i Kanada: Jekonomika, politika, kul'tura, 2011, no. 3, p. 213-228.

96. Zonova T. Publichnaja diplomatija i ee aktory. http://russiancouncil.ru/inner/?id_4=681#top (accessed 12.03.13)

Table. Models of contemporary public diplomacy

Country	USA	China	Russian Federation
Events that have boosted the public diplomacy	Terrorist attacks of September 11, 2001	Tiananmen Square protests of 1989	Ukraine Orange Revolution of 2004
Institutions	1.United States Information Agency (1953-1999) 2. Bureau of Public Affaires 3.Inter-ministerial Committee for International Policy 4.Audiovisual Department 5. Coordination Inter-ministerial Committee for Public Diplomacy and Strategic Communication (2006 – present).	1.Advertising Department (2003-present) 2.State Council Information Office – the supreme authority of the Chinese public diplomacy 3. State Council Office of the External Advertising.	1. Ministry of Foreign Affairs, Roszarubejtsentr – Russian Center for international scientific and cultural cooperation (1994) 2. Rossotrudnecestvo – Federal Agency for CIS problems, of the citizens who live abroad, and of international cooperation (2008) 3. Ministry of Regional Development 4.'Obcestvennaia Palata'.
Public diplomacy's current goals	1.USA image – a state of hopes and opportunities, 2. Collaborate with the allies to isolate and marginalize the violent extremists who threaten the liberty, 3. Develop common values and interests of Americans and other peoples.	1. China – a state which aspires to offer a better future to its people, and searches ways to make the political system better understood. 2. China – a stable, responsible and reliable economic partner. Aspires to be seen as an economic power. 3. Chinese leaders – responsible and reliable members for the	1.Creat a favorable image abroad, 2. Defend and recognize the Russian citizens and compatriots rights from abroad, 3.Broaden the communication area of Russian language and culture, 4.Consolidate the organizations of compatriots, 5.Prevent the

		international community.	reinterpretation of the history in the post-soviet space.
Documents	1.National Security Strategy of the United States (2002). 2.U.S. National Strategy for Public Diplomacy and Strategic Communication (2007) 3.Strategic Communication to combat the ideological support for terrorism (2007) 4. Development strategic plan of informational technologies in 2011 – 2013: the digital diplomacy	1.White Book (2005)	1.Foreign Policy Concept (2000) 2. Overview of Russian Federation foreign policy (2007) 3.Foreign policy concept (2008)
Means for achieving	1.Cultural diplomacy 2.Cultural and educational exchange programs (Fulbright program) 3. Media Radio American Voice Radio Free Europe CNN 4. Internet	1.Public declarations 2.Cultural diplomacy Confucius Institute (since 2004) 3.Educational programs (since 2004) 4. Media Xinhua networks – official press agency China Daily (1981) Radio China International CCTV	1.Cultural diplomacy Russchii Mir 2.Media Russia Today (2005) Rusia ali Laum(2007) Russian Gazeta (2007) Russia in Global Affairs 2.Runet (Russian version of Internet) 3.Russian Orthodox Church

Lightning Source UK Ltd.
Milton Keynes UK
UKHW010643080421
381649UK00001B/79